W9-CBP-853

WHY AMERICA NEEDS RELIGION

W Farwell '96

Why America Needs Religion

Secular Modernity and Its Discontents

Guenter Lewy

William B. Eerdmans Publishing Company
Grand Rapids, Michigan / Cambridge, U.K.

© 1996 Wm. B. Eerdmans Publishing Co.
255 Jefferson Ave. S.E., Grand Rapids, Michigan 49503 /
P.O. Box 163, Cambridge CB3 9PU U.K.

Printed in the United States of America

01 00 99 98 97 96   7 6 5 4 3 2 1

Library of Congress Cataloging-in-Publication Data

Lewy, Guenter.
    Why America needs religion: secular modernity and its discontents /
Guenter Lewy.
        p.   cm.
    Includes bibliographical references.
    ISBN 0-8028-4162-7 (pbk.: alk. paper)
    1. Christianity — United States. 2. Secularism — United States.
3. United States — Moral conditions. 4. Religion and ethics.
5. Christianity and culture. I. Title.
BR515.G84   1996
277.3′0829 — dc20   96-9149
                                                 CIP

Contents

v

To propose that securing civil virtue is the purpose of religion is blasphemous. To deny that securing civil virtue is a benefit of religion is blindness.

Statement, "Evangelicals and Catholics Together: The Christian Mission in the Third Millennium," May 1994

Preface

This book deals with the crisis of secular modernity and the relevance and contribution of the Christian religion to America's moral life. Since I am neither a Christian nor a theist, some remarks about why I undertook this project and how it evolved during the course of my writing may be of interest to the reader.

For some time now, prominent American religious thinkers have argued that the real challenge of our age — an age of secularism — is not the threat of war or of economic decline but the crisis of unbelief. According to their argument, the severance of morality from fixed values and standards, the discarding of theological sanctions, has created a situation of moral anarchy in which everything is permitted. The grim statistics of violence, broken homes, out-of-wedlock births, alcohol abuse, drug addiction, and so on are held up as the outward manifestations of a moral crisis rooted in the rejection of God. The prevalence of secular humanism and moral relativism are said to have undermined the meaning and significance of human life, to have created a debased world of modernity in which there are no firm values and nothing is either absolutely right or absolutely wrong.

I started this book with the intention of refuting this thesis. For most of my adult life, I had lived with the view that ethical beliefs are a matter of personal commitment and cannot be regarded as true or false. I had become impressed by the rigor of analytic philosophy and by Wittgenstein's assertion that "philosophy is a battle against the bewitchment of our intelligence by means of language." Hence, the emphasis of contemporary philosophers on analyzing the language of morals — the terms and concepts used in moral reasoning — seemed to me highly appropriate. This was the way to move forward toward a sounder and more rational morality.

The diversity of moral beliefs and ways of life seemed to me to require acceptance of the idea of ethical and cultural relativism; the impossibility of adjudicating between these diverse practices dictated a noncognitivist approach to ethics — that is, it implied the impossibility of knowing what constituted moral truth. I scoffed at the argument made by religious thinkers such as Richard John Neuhaus, Carl F. H. Henry, and Francis A. Schaeffer that this approach led necessarily to an abdication of moral judgment and nihilism. An admirer of the Enlightenment and Freud, I regarded religion not only as an arbitrary invention born out of human weakness but also as unnecessary for leading a moral life. The son of non-observant German Jews, I thought of myself as a secular humanist; relativism was a safeguard against intolerance and moral arrogance. American society had its share of violence and moral depravity, but how could unbelief be responsible for this state of affairs when so many people attended church services and voiced their belief in God? On the other hand, I thought, how could decent persons such as John Dewey and Sidney Hook, although committed to a philosophy of secular humanism, be blamed for a moral crisis that they abhorred as much as every preacher of the Word of God? Was not the theme of a moral crisis as old as human civilization itself, and did it not predate the emergence of the very notion of secularism? Had not the Hebrew prophets sounded the same alarm now raised by the Billy Grahams and Jerry Falwells of American society? Were not some of the most vocal critics of secular humanism religious bigots and corrupt preachers whose aims boded ill for the cherished American ideal of the separation of church and state? In short, I considered the attack on secular modernity to be a danger to individual liberty as well as an affront to people of goodwill who happened to be agnostics or atheists.

A funny thing, if one can call it that, happened on the way to the completion of this book, which I envisaged as a defense of secular humanism and ethical relativism. Positions that I had always supported and taken for granted turned out to be, on new reflection, far less convincing than I had assumed. This change in my outlook began with the realization that with regard to certain crucial moral issues concerning the meaning of life and death, I had more in common with religious moralists such as James A. Gustafson, Paul Ramsey, and Richard A. McCormick than with most secular humanists. I found much of the writing of the analytic philosophers, to the extent that they at all tackled substantive moral questions such as euthanasia and abortion, arid hair-splitting that was of little help in the resolution of urgent moral dilemmas. Concentration on the language of morals and on the logic of moral reasoning had trivialized the subject of ethics. For example, articles I encountered in my reading on the subject of abortion that had such titles as "Do Zygots Become People?" and "Later Selves and Moral Principles" seemed to me rather unhelpful, to put it charitably. Many of these articles are populated by kittens, chimps, Martians, talking dogs, and other esoteric creatures — everything but human fetuses growing in the wombs of real women. On the other hand, much of the best writing on the burning moral issues of our day made no reference at all to the kind of methodological (meta-ethical) questions I had always been preoccupied with, such as how to justify or prove moral judgments.

My dissatisfaction with the linguistic minuets performed by analytic philosophers, my lack of agreement with the moral positions taken by many secular humanists, and my attraction to those embraced by some prestigious Christian theologians raised questions such as these: Was there something in the very nature of secular humanism that led to what I considered morally unacceptable views? What role does or can religion play in elucidating, confirming, and supporting moral beliefs and conduct?

The title of this book reveals my overall conclusion as well as my focus on contemporary American society. Inasmuch as at least 86 percent of Americans consider themselves Christians, I talk about Christianity for the most part, instead of dealing with religion in general. This concentration on the religion of the great majority of the American people does not reflect disrepect for the worth and contribution of other religions to moral discourse but simply represents the recognition of a sociological reality.

In the introductory chapter, conceived as a historical prologue, I examine the disagreement between those who have seen Christianity as the source of moral inspiration for Western civilization and those who have condemned it as a force for intolerance and ignorance. In Chapter 2 I look at the ambiguous legacy of the Enlightenment and trace the rise of secularism. Chapter 3 is my description of some of the destructive consequences of the modern, secularist mind-set such as the crisis of the monogamous family and the related problem of the inner-city underclass. In Chapters 4 and 5 I present an empirical report card on the questions of whether America is becoming a more secular society and of whether the conduct of believing Christians with regard to crime, out-of-wedlock births, and other indices of social disorder is different from that of less religious individuals. These questions have often been the subject of anecdotal reporting; the large quantity of empirical data in existence has been neglected. In Chapter 6, the conclusion, I discuss the role of moral education and of the churches in achieving moral renewal. I also outline my own personal view of the relationship between religion and morality.

I end this intellectual journey with some of my previously held ideas intact and many others discarded. I remain a religious agnostic, but, unlike most atheists, I not only am not hostile to traditional religion but consider it a highly valuable, not to say essential, social institution. I am convinced that the moral regeneration and repair of a frayed social fabric that this country so badly needs will not take place unless more people take their religion seriously. I continue to question the claim pressed by many Christian theologians that they have a hold on moral Truth, yet I find myself in agreement with not a few of their moral positions — my appreciation of the Judeo-Christian moral heritage goes beyond its social usefulness. Useful or not, widely accepted or contested, many precepts of this moral heritage have assumed a new importance in my moral outlook. In sum, in this book I argue for the central role of religion in providing society and its members with a moral anchor. The urgent task for believers and nonbelievers alike, I submit, is to replenish the moral capital that was accumulated over many centuries from a unique stock of religious and ethical teachings, a fund of treasure that we have been depleting of late at an alarming rate.

GUENTER LEWY

1. Christianity and Western Civilization: A Historical Prologue

The contribution of Christianity to the development of Western civilization and the moral life of the West has been a subject of debate at least since the Renaissance. There are those who see Christianity as the principal source of the West's spiritual values, especially of the ideas of individual dignity, human brotherhood, and social justice, a standard of right above mere human enactments. "It is Christian culture," writes Christopher Dawson, "that has created Western man and the Western way of life."[1] The modern doctrine of individualism, argues Herbert Butterfield, derives from the Christian belief "that men are spiritual beings, born for eternity, and having a value incommensurate with that of everything else in the created universe."[2]

A quite different assessment of Christianity emerged during the Enlightenment of the eighteenth century. Although accepting the basic goodness of Christian ethics, some thinkers maintained that because of the villainy and corruption of its priesthood, Christianity had failed to realize the values of the Christian gospel. Still others, mounting a far more radical attack, rejected the very essence of Christian morality and branded the Old and New Testaments a collection of childish absurdities and rustic superstitions. For Voltaire, revealed religion was a disease; the history of Christianity was a history of fanaticism and cruelty. The same sentiments have been voiced by more recent thinkers. At the end of the nineteenth century, Nietzsche called Chris-

---

1. Dawson, *The Historical Reality of Christian Culture: A Way to the Renewal of Human Life* (New York: Harper and Brothers, 1960), p. 255.
2. Butterfield, *Writings on Christianity and History*, ed. C. T. McIntyre (New York: Oxford University Press, 1979), p. 40.

1

tianity a curse and depravity, "the *one* immortal blemish of mankind."[3] Bertrand Russell has been hardly less scathing in his condemnation: "The whole contention that Christianity has had an elevating moral influence can only be maintained by wholesale ignoring or falsification of the historical evidence." If modern Christianity did less harm than it used to do in the Middle Ages, this was so only because it was less fervently believed. "I say quite deliberately," Russell concluded, "that the Christian religion, as organized in its churches, has been and still is the principal enemy of moral progress in the world."[4]

Both those who consider Christianity the inspiration of Western values and those who regard it as the embodiment of irrationality and moral regress have argued their case like lawyers who present briefs for their clients. They have marshalled whatever evidence would support their position, and they have ignored whatever facts tended to put their opponent in a good light. Disregarding the more simplistic rhetoric, I propose in this chapter to look at some of the more important issues that have figured in this debate and to examine the possibility of arriving at a moral balance sheet.

The Case against Christianity

That organized Christianity has often given rise to intolerance, persecution, and bigotry is a generally accepted historical fact. The torture and burning of heretics by the medieval Inquisitors and the witch-hunting craze of the fifteenth and sixteenth centuries are only the best-known instances of a record of evildoing that no Christian acquainted with the past can deny. The learned English Catholic Lord Acton called the church's attitude toward unbelievers, heretics, savages, and witches a blemish that could not be ignored or erased and "the principal obstacle on the way to Rome."[5] The real question, therefore, is not whether the church is responsible for these awful deeds but whether this catalogue of horrors represents an aberration born of human weakness or a logical result of Christian teachings. Were the

3. Nietzsche, *The Antichrist*, p. 62, cited by Charles M. Natoli in *Nietzsche and Pascal on Christianity* (New York: Peter Lang, 1985), p. 82.

4. Russell, *Why I Am Not a Christian and Other Essays* (New York: Simon & Schuster, 1964), pp. 202, 199, 21.

5. Lord Acton in a letter to Mary Gladstone, cited by G. G. Coulton in *Inquisition and Liberty* (Boston: Beacon Press, 1959), p. 315.

stake, the gibbet, the rack, and the ghetto — symbols of our inhumanity in the name of God — the results of institutional failure, a corruption of the Christian gospel of love, or were they the necessary consequence of Christian doctrine, prominently including the Christian claim to be the only true faith?

The repression of pagan religions and Christian heresies began during the fourth Christian century under Theodosius I, who made Christianity the established religion of the Roman Empire. Some of the church fathers were opposed to religious coercion. Saint Gregory of Nyssa insisted that "the use of violence to force acceptance of the Gospel would be contrary to man's dignity; because man's freedom is what constitutes his likeness to God."[6] Others rejected state intervention in spiritual matters, while still others objected merely to the imposition of the death penalty. By the the twelfth century, with heresies such as those of the Cathari spreading, the repression of heresy by force had come to be taken for granted. Heretics would be put before an ecclesiastical tribunal, and, in accordance with the papal bull *Ad extirpanda* issued in 1252, they were often tortured in an attempt to get them to confess or name other heretics. Those who refused to repent or relapsed into heresy after repentance were handed over to the secular government to be burnt at the stake.

Under Pope Innocent III, a permanent papal tribunal, the Inquisition, was set up. It was made up of Dominican friars who worked in collaboration with local bishops. There exist no firm figures on the number of persons tortured and/or burned. The Spanish Inquisition, established in 1482, is said to have burned 31,000 Protestants and Jews, but this figure is contested. While acquittal was rare, most of the victims were not put to death but received penalties such as lengthy imprisonment and the confiscation of property. The methods of torture, too, were on the whole less severe than those used by secular governments. Still, there can be little doubt that the medieval Inquisition caused vast suffering, and this dark chapter in the history of Christianity did not end with the coming of the Reformation. Quite the contrary: for a time the intensification of religious passion added new fury to the spirit of persecution, and Protestants showed themselves capable of the same enormities they earlier had charged their Catholic opponents with committing.

6. Gregory of Nyssa, cited by A. F. Carillo de Albornoz in *Religious Liberty*, trans. John Drury (New York: Sheed & Ward, 1967), p. 28.

The religious fervor of the Reformation also led to the intensification of witch-hunting, which soon claimed thousands of victims, most of them women. Torture was widely used to obtain confessions and elicit new accusations. It is estimated that between the years 1500 and 1700 more than 50,000 people were executed as witches; it was only the spread of scientific thinking in the eighteenth century that finally put an end to this craze. The last legal execution of a witch took place in Protestant Switzerland in 1782; the last Spanish execution for heresy was in 1826.[7]

The historical record leaves little doubt that both the Inquisition and the witchcraft epidemic derived their justification from theological premises. The Dominican friars who administered the Inquisition have been described as "men of child-like humility and even tender sensitiveness";[8] they were learned men rather than bloodthirsty sadists. Most basically, the willingness to use force against unbelievers, heretics, and witches stemmed from the firm conviction that there was only one religious truth and that the correct theological opinion was essential to salvation. As the English historian W. E. H. Lecky has noted,

> If men believe with an intense and realizing faith that their own view of a disputed question is true beyond all possibility of mistake, if they further believe that those who adopt other views will be doomed by the Almighty to an eternity of misery which, with the same moral disposition but with a different belief, they would have escaped, these men will, sooner or later, persecute to the full extent of their power. . . . What suffering that man can inflict can be comparable to the eternal misery of all who embrace the doctrine of the heretic?[9]

If we add to this the conviction of medieval people that heretics were debased individuals who constituted a threat to social stability, we have all the elements that justify the practice of persecution and religious coercion. Convenient texts could then be produced from the Old and New Testaments to prove not only the justification but the

---

7. Joseph Klaits, *Servants of Satan: The Age of the Witch Hunts* (Bloomington: Indiana University Press, 1985), pp. 164-67; Paul Johnson, *A History of Christianity* (New York: Atheneum, 1977), p. 308.

8. Erich Przywara, quoted by Reinhold Niebuhr in vol. 2 of *The Nature and Destiny of Man* (New York: Charles Scribner's Sons, 1943), p. 221.

9. Lecky, *History of the Rise and Influence of the Spirit of Rationalism in Europe*, vol. 2 (New York: D. Appleton, 1866), p. 12.

necessity of proceeding with vigor against religious dissenters. It was Saint Augustine who first drew attention to the saying of Luke 14:23: "Compel people to come in." The learned saint argued that it was merciful to punish heretics, even by death, if this could save them or others from the eternal suffering that awaited the unconverted. Several centuries later, Saint Thomas Aquinas similarly emphasized that heretics deserved not only to be separated from the church but to be eliminated from the world by death. In support of this view, he quoted Saint Jerome: "The tainted flesh must be cut away, and the infected sheep cast out from the fold: lest the whole house burn, the mass be corrupted, the body become infected and the flock perish."[10] Both Catholics and Protestants upheld the duty of executing witches by invoking the injunction of Exodus 22:18: "Thou shall not suffer a witch to live."

Religious persecution ceased first as a result of secular considerations; only much later did religious toleration and religious liberty receive theological blessing. It is a fact, Herbert Butterfield concedes, "that the Christian Church began a cruel policy of persecution from the earliest moment when it was in a position (and had the power) to do so." Both Catholics and Protestants, he points out, refrained from persecution only after churchmen lost the right to govern and after their warfare against each other had resulted in total exhaustion.[11] Protestants were first to accept the principle of religious liberty. The Catholic Church did not embrace it formally until Vatican Council II.

The Declaration on Religious Freedom *(Dignitatis Humanae)*, approved by the Council in December 1965, acknowledged that in the life of the church "there have at times appeared ways of acting which were less in accord with the spirit of the Gospel and even opposed to it" (no. 12). Indeed, the Declaration noted, "Revelation does not affirm in so many words the right of man to immunity from external coercion in matters religious" (no. 9).[12] This fact, a commentator has noted, "explains how many Christian theologians, whose orthodoxy was beyond question, could have been opposed to religious freedom throughout the course of history."[13] Nevertheless, the Council now did

10. Saint Thomas Aquinas, *Summa Theologica*, II, 2, 14, q.11, a.3.

11. Butterfield, *Christianity and History* (New York: Charles Scribner's Sons, 1950), p. 132.

12. Walter M. Abbott, ed., *The Documents of Vatican II* (New York: America Press, 1966), p. 688.

13. De Albornoz, *Religious Liberty*, p. 39.

affirm that the right to religious liberty had its roots in the Gospel's espousal of human dignity; "the requirements of human dignity have come to be more adequately known to human reason through centuries of experience" (no. 9). In a letter issued on 14 November 1994, preparing the Catholic Church for the "Great Jubilee" in the year 2000 that will mark the third millennium of Christianity, Pope John Paul II urged atonement for past transgressions, including "acquiescence given, especially in certain centuries, to intolerance and even the use of violence in the service of truth."[14] Belatedly, the Catholic Church has thus put behind it repressive methods and inquisitorial practices which, as a German Catholic theologian has put it, "should make the true Christian blush for shame."[15]

Vatican Council II also denounced anti-Semitism. For centuries the church had relegated Jews to an inferior position as punishment for having killed Christ and for their obstinacy in refusing to acknowledge the truth of Christianity. Earlier church councils had forbidden marriage between Jews and Christians, had forbidden Jews to employ Christian servants, had disqualified them from holding public office, had forced them into ghettos, and had required them to wear distinctive dress — all measures later reenacted by Hitler's government in Germany. Indeed, most scholars agree that modern anti-Semitism, which culminated in the Nazi murder of millions of Jews, would have been impossible without the deep-rooted attitude of hostility toward the Jews engendered during centuries of Christian defamation.[16] The charge of deicide was the rallying cry for numerous pogroms against Jews, with monks and local clergy often leading the mob. No pope ever lent support to acts of violence against Jews, and some sought to protect them. But church teaching for centuries vilified the Jews as accursed by God and thus prepared the ground for the violence that did occur. The early Protestant reformers continued this legacy of hatred. In a pamphlet entitled "On the Jews and Their Lies," Martin Luther denounced the Jews as "a brood of vipers and children of the devil" who get rich by means of usury, poison wells, murder Christian children, and curse Jesus Christ. He recommended that their synagogues,

14. Alan Cowell, "Pope Wants the Church to Atone for Historical Errors," *New York Times*, 15 November 1994.

15. Albert Hartmann, *Toleranz und Christlicher Glaube* (Frankfurt/Main: Knecht 1955), p. 222, cited by de Albornoz in *Religious Liberty*, p. 52.

16. Cf. Gavin I. Langmuir, *History, Religion, and Antisemitism* (Berkeley and Los Angeles: University of California Press, 1990), p. 40.

schools, and houses be razed. If they did not give up usury and learn to "earn their bread in the sweat of their brow," he urged that they be expelled from the country.[17] The Nazis reissued this pamphlet in a popular edition in 1935.[18]

In the Declaration on the Relationship of the Church to Non-Christian Religions *(Nostra Aetate)*, Vatican Council II affirmed that "the Jews should not be presented as repudiated or cursed by God, as if such views followed from the holy Scripture." Mindful of its common patrimony with Jews, the declaration continued, the church "deplores the hatred, persecutions, and displays of anti-Semitism directed against the Jews at any time and from any source" (no. 4).[19] In 1990, Pope John Paul II endorsed a statement acknowledging that some aspects of Christian teaching and practice had fostered anti-Semitism, called it "a sin against God and humanity," and declared that the church should repent for the anti-Semitism that had found a place in Catholic thought and behavior.[20] Such statements of contrition for past misdeeds have been generally welcomed, though they have also provided new support for those who had argued all along that Christianity constituted an immoral and retrograde force in human history.

Other charges against Christianity include its alleged attitude of antipathy toward women and its deep suspicion of sex. Greek and Jewish ideas and practices, which confined women to a position of inferiority and demanded rigorous control of sexual conduct, became linked with the ascetic temper strongly present in early Christianity. The result, it has been argued, was to create an image of women as a source of temptation for men and to foster disdain for the body and sexual pleasure; these teachings are said to have blighted the lives of uncounted Christians in the past. Citing the Catholic prohibition of divorce and birth control, Sidney Hook called historic Christianity a force opposed to enlightened morality. "When one considers the ocean of tears that have been shed by suffering mankind, especially

---

17. Luther, "On the Jews and Their Lies," in vol. 2 of *Luther's Works* (Philadelphia: Fortress Press, 1971), pp. 265, 268, 272, 277.

18. Luther's diatribe against the Jews was often cited in Nazi propaganda. For example, the Nazi Office of Racial Policy *(Rassenpolitisches Amt)* published excerpts from Luther's book in its *Informationsdienst* of 30 November and 10 December 1938. Cf. Robert Proctor, *Racial Hygiene: Medicine under the Nazis* (Cambridge, Mass.: Harvard University Press, 1988), p. 88.

19. Abbott, *The Documents of Vatican II*, pp. 666-67.

20. Peter Steinfels, "Pope Endorses Statement on Antisemitism," *New York Times*, 7 December 1990.

WHO DEFINES HUMANITY?

womankind, because of the inhumanity of laws directly attributable to the influence of religious dogmas," he wrote, "it is hard to find any compensating consideration."[21]

At a time of widespread sexual laxity, rampant teenage pregnancies, and deadly diseases, many of them contracted during the course of a promiscuous lifestyle, Hook's harsh judgment, pronounced more than twenty-five years ago, does not quite ring true. The control of the sexual impulse, derived from Christian belief, today not only has survival value but, as many mental health professionals see it, may actually enhance human fulfillment. Moreover, it should be remembered that the Catholic Church played an important role in the emergence of the modern consensual marriage, a relationship based on the freely given consent of both man and woman. The matrimonial contract came to be a sacrament and as such could be received only by individuals acting voluntarily. In turn, the principle of consent accepted for marriage strengthened the idea of individual dignity and self-determination. Furthermore, the Catholic Church encouraged greater respect for women by opposing concubinage, adultery, and divorce at the whim of the man.[22] Here, as in many other aspects of life, it is necessary to beware of one-sided polemics and to recognize the many different consequences of religious teachings.

The Case for Christianity

The immorality and decadence of Roman society during the first three centuries of the Common Era have often been exaggerated, but there is no denying that imperial Rome, just as ancient Greece earlier, was characterized by an appalling disregard for human life. Even if we ignore the routine resort to abortion, a procedure which remains the subject of moral disagreement, the common practice of abandoning weak or deformed infants will find few defenders. Many of these babies perished; others were picked up by speculators who raised them as slaves or prostitutes; some were maimed so that they could make money as

---

21. Hook, *The Place of Religion in a Free Society* (Lincoln, Neb.: University of Nebraska Press, 1967), p. 20.

22. Cf. Frances and Joseph Gies, *Marriage and the Family in the Middle Ages* (New York: Harper & Row, 1987). See also Jack Goody, *The Development of the Family and Marriage in Europe* (Cambridge: Cambridge University Press, 1983), pp. 151-55.

beggars for their masters.[23] The life of barbarians, slaves, and captives of war was cheap. Romans amused themselves by watching these social castoffs in gladiatorial contests in which the losers were routinely killed. By contrast, Christianity affirmed the fraternity of all human beings in Christ and insisted that to kill a human being was to usurp God's right to decide who shall live and who shall die. The severity of the crime of causing the death of an infant was magnified by the belief that children who died unbaptized were doomed to eternal perdition. Surveying this period, the English historian Lecky, not given to pro-Christian bias, concluded that Christianity, by dogmatically asserting the sinfulness of all destruction of human life as a matter of simple convenience or amusement, "formed a new standard higher than any which then existed in the world." The "first and most manifest duty of a Christian man was to look upon his fellow-men as sacred beings, and from this notion grew up the eminently Christian idea of the sanctity of all human life."[24] Today this concept is part of the ethos of Western civilization.

In ancient pagan society there was little concern for the victims of violence and injustice. There was no reason why Zeus or Jupiter should feel sorry for slaves or other victims of misfortune. Christianity, on the other hand, told of a God who cared deeply about his children. The Gospel of Jesus Christ contains eloquent passages enjoining the feeding of the hungry, the clothing of the naked, the visiting of the sick and imprisoned, and the kind treatment of the stranger (Matt. 25:34-40). Much of this teaching had its roots in Judaism, out of which Christianity emerged. The Hebrew prophets had preached justice for the poor and oppressed, and Christianity continued teaching the moral duty of showing compassion for the impoverished, sick, aged, and enslaved everywhere. It was a universal religion for all humankind. To love God and to be Christlike was to love one's neighbor as well as the unlovely and unlovable. To be good meant to be benevolent. Charity became a basic virtue.

Christians consequently organized the first public hospitals, asylums for lepers, and refuges for strangers. Christian congregations pro-

23. Cf. John Boswell, *The Kindness of Strangers: The Abandonment of Children in Western Europe from Late Antiquity to the Renaissance* (New York: Pantheon, 1988), p. 113.

24. Lecky, *History of European Morals from Augustus to Charlemagne*, vol. 2 (New York: George Braziller, 1955), pp. 20, 18.

vided help for widows and orphans, the sick and disabled, as well as relief for the poor. In pagan Rome, gift-giving had been an act of politics; for the Christian church, it became an act of mercy. For the first time, the historian Peter Brown stresses, women took on a "public role, in their own right, in relation to the poor: they gave alms in person, they visited the sick, they founded shrines and poorhouses."[25] To be sure, since charity was linked to penance and the cleansing of the conscience from minor faults, many gave money to the poor out of selfish motives — to derive spiritual benefits for themselves — rather than out of regard for the welfare of the deprived. One should also beware of idealizing an age that was often violent and brutal and little given to lovingkindness. Many monasteries and members of the clergy dishonored the Christian gospel of love by their meanness and corruption. Still, amid all the failings that have defaced the church, there were those such as Saint Francis and Saint Teresa, as well as countless others whose names are not remembered, who served God by caring for the unfortunates of this world. Indeed, after criticizing organized Christianity for its fanaticism and persecution of dissenters, Lecky expressed his admiration for the unique achievement of Christianity in promoting charity: "For the first time in the history of mankind, it has inspired many thousands of men and women, at the sacrifice of all worldly interests, and often under circumstances of extreme discomfort or danger, to devote their entire lives to the single object of assuaging the sufferings of humanity."[26]

Acts of charity did not remain limited to the monastic clergy. In the eighteenth century, seeking to copy the life of the early church, John Wesley, the founder of Methodism, sent his followers to visit the sick of London and started the first free dispensaries for medications as well as a widows' home. In America too, from early on, acts of compassion and programs of charity had a religious underpinning. In the nineteenth century, the Salvation Army and Young Men's and Women's Christian Associations addressed the needs of the poor and destitute in the burgeoning cities. As Marvin Olasky has shown in an important study, *The Tragedy of American Compassion*, these religiously inspired organizations linked charity to the reformation of character; in this way they were able to avoid suppressing the instinct of self-reliance and encouraging dependency, two consequences of many

25. Brown, *The Cult of the Saints: Its Rise and Function in Latin Christianity* (Chicago: University of Chicago Press, 1981), p. 46.
26. Lecky, *History of European Morals*, p. 85.

social programs instituted by the modern welfare state.[27] The development of a kinder and more compassionate society has been aided by secular reform movements such as British utilitarianism, but there is no denying that the introduction of social services and the idea of social justice owe a decisive debt to the Christian conception of love. To this day, religious congregations — many members of the clergy as well as numerous individual Christians — devote their lives to those who are homeless, addicted, and/or afflicted with disease.

Sensitivity to the suffering of others has been nourished by obedience to the imperative of self-sacrificing love taught by Jesus and by the recollection of the suffering of Christ. It therefore will come as no surprise that many of those who rescued Jews during the Holocaust of World War II were religiously motivated. It is estimated that about 50,000 Christians saved about 200,000 Jews. Informed by the Christian religion, many of the rescuers believed in the common humanity of all people; others regarded the Jews as the people of God, to whom Christians had a special obligation. The sociologist Samuel Oliner, himself a survivor who studied rescuers of Jews, states that religiosity was only weakly related to rescue efforts. At the same time, he found among a majority of rescuers the firm belief that justice is not merely for oneself or one's own group but for all. The role model of caring parents was also important; the rescuers had clearly been taught certain values. Such values would, of course, have been inculcated by religious upbringing, which 90 percent of the rescuers had.[28]

A Dutchman who hid Jews from the Nazis later explained to his son, today a minister in Michigan, his reasons for rescuing Jews: "As God shows compassion to us, so we must show compassion to others."[29] Perhaps the most outstanding example of selfless conduct was the rescue work by Pastor André Trocmé and his Protestant parishioners in the village of Le Chambon-sur-Lignon in Southern France: they sheltered about 5,000 Jews. Awareness of the suffering of their Huguenot forefathers probably gave the 3,000 people in this commune a special sensitivity to the suffering of the Jews. However, it was their religious faith, especially the command to "love thy neighbor as thyself," that became a crucial component of their heroic con-

27. Cf. Olasky, *The Tragedy of American Compassion* (Washington, D.C.: Regnery Gateway, 1992).
28. Samuel P. and Pearl M. Oliner, *The Altruistic Personality: Rescuers of Jews in Nazi Europe* (New York: Free Press, 1988), p. 156.
29. Quoted in Olasky, *The Tragedy of American Compassion*, p. 231.

duct. Most of them, it appears, did not have to search their souls over the decision to help the persecuted Jews. They made a revealing comment to French filmmaker Pierre Sauvage, who produced a film about these courageous people entitled *Weapons of the Spirit*: "Those who agonize do not act; those who act do not agonize."[30]

Throughout its history, Christianity has made moral teaching one of the key functions of its clergy; moral dispositions became the necessary condition for the due performance of religious rites and for participation in the sacraments. Although many times the principles of right conduct were more violated than observed, the emphasis on moral self-improvement left Christians with a sense of guilt that often led to the abandonment of vices such as drunkenness and debauchery. During the nineteenth century, religious revivals, religiously motivated temperance movements, and Sunday-school instruction all had in common a desire to encourage improvement of character, especially inner control and self-discipline. "In myriad ways but with extraordinary singleness of purpose," write two students of the causes of crime, "Americans (and Englishmen) in the mid-nineteenth century invested heavily in programs designed to inculcate self-control and thereby enhance character. These efforts were directed at what reformers took to be the causes of crime and disorder — impulsiveness and a lack of conscience." Despite rapid industrialization, urbanization, immigration, and a widening gulf between the social classes, these endeavors showed results. "The most striking difference in outlook between those days and the contemporary period," they note, "is that the broadly based effort at moral uplift, and the religious convictions of those elites who led and sustained it, have been weakened and abandoned."[31]

Ambivalence and Moral Ambiguity

The effort to arrive at a balance sheet for the moral record of Christianity is complicated by the fact that in many instances Christianity both abetted and helped overcome human evil. A case in point is the attitude of Christianity toward slavery. We find in Christian teachings ample

30. For a good account of the rescue work of Le Chambon, see Philip H. Hallie's *Lest Innocent Blood Be Shed: The Story of the Village of Le Chambon and How Goodness Happened There* (New York: Harper & Row, 1979).

31. James Q. Wilson and Richard J. Herrnstein, *Crime and Human Nature* (New York: Simon & Schuster, 1985), p. 434.

support for the institution of slavery but also ideals that encouraged emancipation and inspired the ardor of the abolitionist movement.

Jesus lived in a world where slavery was common, and the teachings of early Christianity, like those of the Old Testament, took the institution of slavery for granted. Slaveholders throughout history have been fond of quoting passages from the Gospels that call upon slaves to be obedient to their masters and willingly to accept pain and suffering.[32] At the same time, the New Testament emphasizes the basic dignity and equality of all human beings. Since the coming of Christ, Paul told the Galatians in what has been called the Magna Carta of Christian liberty, all humans are the children of God: "There is neither Jew nor Greek, there is neither slave nor free, there is neither male nor female; for you are all one in Christ Jesus" (3:28). This was not a call for social equality but an affirmation of equal worth. Still, this stress on the essential kinship of all men and women, anticipated by the Roman Stoics, eventually was to have truly revolutionary consequences.

The church fathers saw slavery as a consequence of as well as a penalty for sin, and they too exhorted slaves to obey even the harshest masters. For many centuries, popes, bishops, monasteries, and individual priests continued to own slaves. The church encouraged the manumission of slaves and praised it as a meritorious deed, but throughout the Middle Ages the church also supported the severe punishment of those who sought to escape bondage. By the fifteenth century, the enslavement of men from Christian countries was looked down upon and so had become rare, but this negative attitude toward slavery did not extend to unbelievers. When Europeans seized or purchased infidels, they saw themselves as dealing a blow to unbelief as well as saving souls. In 1488, Pope Innocent VIII accepted the gift of one hundred Moors from King Ferdinand of Spain and distributed them among the cardinals and nobility.[33]

The Indians of the New World at first were abused and enslaved like other infidels. The thirst for gold and the desire to Christianize combined to lead to widespread exploitation and cruelty. But there also were churchmen who protested this mistreatment and who exhorted the colonists to win converts by peaceful means. In a debate at Valladolid

---

32. Colossians 3:22; Ephesians 6:5-8; 1 Corinthians 7:20-24; 1 Timothy 6:1-2; Titus 2:9-10; 1 Peter 2:18-21.

33. David Brion Davis, *The Problem of Slavery in Western Culture* (New York: Oxford University Press, 1988), pp. 100-101.

with the Spanish humanist Juan Gines de Sepulveda held in 1550-51, Bartolomé de Las Casas, bishop of Chiapa in Guatemala, argued against the enslavement of the American Indians by upholding the thesis "All the peoples of the world are men." Legislation promulgated by Philip II in 1573 was influenced by these arguments. The idea that all human beings are equal in the eyes of God and that Christians have a responsibility for the welfare of their brothers and sisters, no matter who they are, had finally become the cutting edge of social reform.[34]

For many years to come, the abandonment of the enslavement of Indians did not benefit black Africans. While it gradually came to be accepted that to deprive Native Americans of their natural liberty constituted a crime, to remove blacks from their harsh world of sin and superstition was seen as an act of liberation. Even Las Casas, who has entered history as "The Protector of the Indians," never publicly condemned the enslavement of blacks and as late as 1544 still owned slaves. In Protestant North America, during most of the colonial era, slavery was an accepted institution. Though human bondage had been brought into the world by sin, the argument ran, it later had become a proper part of the worldly orders of subjection and authority. Christian liberty was held to extend only to the spirit. Even the Quaker-dominated government of Pennsylvania enacted a harsh slave code, and until the first half of the eighteenth century Quaker merchants were involved in importing and selling West Indian blacks. As late as 1841, Roman Catholic Bishop Francis Kenrick, in the first treatise on moral theology for Americans, maintained that it was no sin to own slaves if they were treated in a humane way.[35] Christian preachers admonished masters to lead their slaves toward a Christian life, but the baptism of slaves and their instruction in the Christian faith did not only fulfill a religious duty. As the historian David Brion Davis has pointed out, religious instruction was also intended to help slaves "internalize those precepts of humility, patience, and willing obedience which would allow masters to rule by love instead of force."[36]

Gradually, however, different views were gaining ground.

---

34. Cf. Lewis Hanke, *The Spanish Struggle for Justice in the Conquest of America* (Philadelphia: University of Pennsylvania Press, 1949), pp. 125-30. Las Casas's *In Defense of the Indians* was republished by Northwest Illinois University Press in 1992.

35. John T. Noonan, Jr., "Development in Moral Doctrine," *Theological Studies* 54 (1993): 667.

36. Davis, *The Problem of Slavery in Western Culture*, p. 203.

Quakers were in the forefront of those who maintained that physical slavery, the bondage of the body, and Christian liberty were incompatible. Christ, argued the Quaker George Keith as early as 1693, had died to bring inward and outward liberty. It was the duty of Christians to show compassion to anyone in need. By the time of the American Revolution, virtually all Protestant denominations had adopted an official position against slavery, but as the production of cotton expanded, this stance began to erode. By the time of the Civil War, every major Protestant body had a southern division strongly defending slavery as instituted by God for the better ordering of a sinful world.

If religious arguments could rationalize the institution of slavery, they could also supply strong weapons for the abolitionists. William Wilberforce, the British philanthropist who did more than any other single individual to abolish the slave trade, was powerfully motivated by the evangelical movement started by John Wesley. In America, too, the abolitionist cause from the beginning was fueled by the conviction that slavery was the fundamental Christian sin and that to do away with this outrage was to score a victory over the devil and to usher in a holy commonwealth. John Brown saw himself as God's chosen instrument and avenger of the crime of slavery. Even the Unitarians, who contributed powerfully to the abolitionist cause in New England, at the time invoked biblical arguments. Most slave rebellions, too, were inspired by religious ideas. The best known of these insurrections was led by a preacher, Nat Turner, who had become convinced, as he announced in his proclamation of 1828, that soon the first would be last and the last would be first. Not surprisingly, many slaveholders came to oppose religious instruction for their slaves; the Bible — though it contained statements supporting slavery — was held to contain too many passages calling for escape from bondage.

The powerful role played by Christian ideas in achieving an end to slavery in America is given short shrift by the historian Forrest Wood in his recent book *The Arrogance of Faith*. Wood calls racism "an inherent flaw of the Christian faith." There has been, he writes, "no greater religious force in the dehumanization of humans than Christianity, the self-proclaimed religion of peace, brotherly love, and fellowship."[37] In a review entitled "The Arrogance of History," fellow

37. Wood, *The Arrogance of Faith: Christianity and Race in America from the Colonial Era to the Twentieth Century* (New York: Alfred A. Knopf, 1990), pp. 37, 12.

historian Eugene Genovese denounces Wood's opus as a "dreadful book" that is marred not only by its numerous factual blunders but also by its ideological agenda. "Notwithstanding the centuries-long complicity of the Christian churches in slavery," Genovese points out, "the abolitionists were able to mount an ideological challenge based on Christian theology." It was Christian doctrine that provided the moral ground on the basis of which opponents of involuntary servitude could successfully challenge slavery.[38]

The emergence of scientific thinking provides another illustration of the complex role played by Christianity in the history of the West. We owe to science a longer and healthier life as well as relief from the toil and drudgery that has afflicted all societies until the coming of modernity. If life is affirmed as a value, as it is by practically all of humanity, these achievements represent not only technical progress but also a moral triumph. Religious arguments were invoked to justify both the neglect and the cultivation of scientific knowledge. While Christian theologians for a long time expressed great distrust of reason, later Christian thinkers considered the pursuit of knowledge and the search for truth moral goods in their own right. In particular, the study of nature and its regularities was seen as a means for promoting the glory of God. The part taken by Christianity in the development of science is thus laden with ambiguity.

Early Christianity was characterized by a suspicion of all worldly things and a disdain for rational knowledge. In his Letter to the Colossians, Paul warned his followers against being misled by "philosophy and empty deceit" (2:8), and in his First Letter to the Corinthians, he called the "wisdom of this world" folly in the eyes of God (3:19). In the third century, Tertullian asked rhetorically, "What has Athens to do with Jerusalem, the Academy with the Church?" His answer was, "We have no need for curiosity since Jesus Christ, nor for inquiry since the Evangel!" Philosophy was "idle speculation"; Christians could do without the "stupidities of philosophy."[39] During the early medieval period, the Dark Ages of Europe, clerks in monasteries copied and preserved many of the Greek and

---

38. Genovese, "The Arrogance of History," *New Republic*, 13 August 1990, p. 35.

39. Tertullian, *De Praescript.* 7, quoted by Charles Norris Cochrane in *Christianity and Classical Culture: A Study of Thought and Action from Augustus to Augustine*, rev. ed. (London: Oxford University Press, 1957), p. 222.

Latin classics, but these writings were often denounced as promoting worldliness and sin.

Medieval science was handicapped by the Christian assumption that the purpose of knowledge was the discovery of God's intentions. Theological affirmations barred the acceptance of new insights. The study of medicine in particular was impeded by the religiously grounded prohibition of the dissection of bodies, and by the belief, propagated by the early church fathers, that diseases were due to God's wrath or to diabolical influence. There prevailed a distrust of reliance upon observation and experimentation. But that is not the entire story. The universities of the thirteenth century developed out of cathedral schools; accordingly, almost all of the most influential intellectuals emerging during the revival of learning that occurred during the thirteenth and fourteenth centuries were friars and clergymen. While medieval scholasticism involved the accumulation of much arid knowledge, it also inculcated disciplined thinking. More fundamentally, it was the medieval insistence on the rationality of God that was crucial for the development of modern science. The world, it was believed, had been created by a reasonable God, and the regularities of nature therefore had to be understood on the basis of reason. It was faith in the orderliness of nature, Alfred North Whitehead concluded in a famous essay, "which has made possible the growth of science."[40]

The assumption that nature constitutes an intelligible order was a prerequisite of modern science, but it was Protestantism that supplied another key ingredient — the obligation of intense concentration on secular activity, "good works" that were seen providing evidence of grace. In the mind of the Puritan, reason served as an important curbing device of the passions; this exaltation of reason, as Robert Merton has argued persuasively, "led to a sympathetic attitude toward those activities which demand the constant application of rigorous reasoning." The Puritan ethos identified industriousness with the expenditure of physical energy and the handling of material objects. It equated cloistered contemplation with idleness and encouraged active experimentation. Rationalism and empiricism were, of course, the essence of modern science, and Puritanism promoted both. "Empiricism and rationalism," concludes Merton, "were canonized, beatified, so to

40. Whitehead, *Science and the Modern World* (New York: Macmillan, 1927), p. 27.

speak."[41] Lastly, the break with Rome, like any act of rebellion, necessarily involved an appeal to the right of individuals to think for themselves, and this glorification of the free intellect also helped advance the development of modern natural science.

Almost two thirds of the early members of the Royal Society, which was formally constituted in 1660, were Puritans, even though the Puritans at that time were a minority in the population of England. All of these men were strongly religious. As Robert Boyle saw it, useful knowledge was good in the eyes of God; scientific achievements manifested his glory. Nature was regarded as a mechanical creation, dependent upon the divine will and ascertainable by reason. God was considered the author of all physical laws; partly as a result of this belief, the new science stressed the importance of searching for the laws of nature. The orderliness of nature and its perfect design, testimony to its transcendent creator, called for inquiry with distinct modes of observation and a highly disciplined scientific method.[42] For Isaac Newton, too, the heavens proclaimed God's triumph. God was a creator as well as a watchful master who occasionally corrected the irregularities of the solar system. In short, the scientific revolution of the seventeenth century not only did not mark a break with the Christian view of the world but benefited from the religious convictions of its pioneers.

The happy union of science and religion lasted until well into the eighteenth century. Open conflict between science and theology did not arise until the nineteenth century, when discoveries in geology and the idea of evolution called into question the biblical narrative of creation. Eventually this conflict was alleviated by critical studies of the Bible that rejected the literal inerrancy of the Scriptures. We do not know what the relationship of science and religion will be in the future. Meanwhile, it is clear that the notion of an inevitable conflict

41. Merton, *Science, Technology and Society in Seventeenth-Century England* (New York: Howard Fertig, 1970), pp. 92-93. For an illuminating discussion of what has come to be known as the "Merton thesis," see I. Bernard Cohen, ed., *Puritanism and the Rise of Modern Science: The Merton Thesis* (New Brunswick, N.J.: Rutgers University Press, 1990).

42. Cf. Eugene M. Klaaren, *Religious Origins of Modern Science: Belief in Creation in Seventeenth-Century Thought* (Grand Rapids, Mich.: Wm. B. Eerdmans, 1977), pp. 188-90. See also William B. Glover, *Biblical Origins of Modern Secular Culture: An Essay in the Interpretation of Western History* (Macon, Ga.: Mercer University Press, 1984).

between these two worldviews, argued in positivistic works of the nineteenth century such as A. D. White's *History of the Warfare of Science with Theology in Christendom*, remains unsupported. More importantly, this view ignores the important contribution that Christianity has made to the development of modern science.

The Unattainable Moral Balance Sheet

Many other aspects of life reveal the contradictory influence of Christianity, a source of both progress and regress, advancing as well as hindering the moral improvement of humankind, providing encourage- BY ment and solace but also fostering passivity and fatalism. The down- WHOSE grading of earthly fortunes and reliance on the blessings of the future STDS, ? life many times have led human beings into submissiveness and willing acceptance of exploitation, but the promise of eternal happiness in the world to come has also cast a ray of hope upon the darkest calamities of earthly existence. The "sufferings of this present time," Paul wrote in his Letter to the Romans, "are not worth comparing with the glory that is to be revealed to us" (8:18). Throughout the history of Christianity, the idea of the remedial and providential character of suffering has provided a shield against despair and has enabled untold millions to endure the tribulations of human life.

Christianity has never ceased to bring consolation to the oppressed. Christian teachings about the need to obey the powers that be (Rom. 13:1-7) have inculcated a spirit of subservience, fortified privilege, and helped perpetuate tyranny. At the same time, the command to Christians that they "obey God rather than men" (Acts 5:29) when faced with constituted authority that exceeds its competence has justified disobedience and resistance to injustice. The Christian churches have often supported authoritarian forms of government, but Christianity has also introduced the idea of limited government, the notion that there are some spheres of life outside the reach of secular rulers. The biblical concept of covenant and the idea of the fundamental equality of all individuals in the eyes of God eventually were given political meaning and did much to pave the way for modern democracy.

The Christian doctrine of sin involving the cruel fate of the reprobate condemned to the eternal punishment of hell undoubtedly has often created a sense of fear and dread. It has also attributed to the Christian God an amazing degree of cruelty and thus may have made such cruelties more acceptable in the human sphere as well. The gleeful observation of the twelfth-century Italian theologian Peter Lombard about punishment — that as the elect behold the unspeakable anguish and torture of the impious, they will not grieve, and "their minds will be sated with joy . . . returning thanks for their own freedom"[43] — is hardly in the spirit of love and compassion enjoined by the Sermon on the Mount. At the same time, it was this very teaching about divine judgment and retribution that provided a new motive for virtue and the observance of Christian moral principles. There exists no way of measuring and comparing the positive impact and the negative impact of this doctrine.

One could lengthen this catalogue of good and evil. The idea of predestination can induce moral laxity, but it can also produce extreme moral rigor in those who want to feel certain that they are among the elect. Puritan theology, despite its belief in an all-powerful God, did not paralyze human effort, for the Puritans also believed that God helps those who help themselves. If the ethic of rigorous legalism practiced by the Puritans and early Methodists created a life of guilt and self-denial, it also issued in a constructive self-discipline that in America helped produce the proverbial Yankee individualism. Christianity led medieval society into cruel crusades, but it also gave birth to the doctrine of the just war, which has done much to make armed conflict less brutal and has put restraints upon the recourse to force. The philosopher Leszek Kolakowski has correctly emphasized that we lack the conceptual instruments for measuring the relative amounts of good and evil in human history: "There is no means of reducing the infinite variety of moral and physical evil [and good] to homogeneous quantifiable units."[44]

There is also the problem of separating the moral contributions of Christianity from those of Judaism and Greco-Roman culture, from which many Christian ideas are derived. In modern times, Christian ethics have been enriched by Renaissance humanism and the idea of individual rights linked to the Enlightenment and modern democracy. With a degree of understatement, the historian Crane Brinton, therefore, has called the taxonomy of morals "a difficult business,"[45] and

43. Lombard, *Sentences*, lib. IV, quoted in vol. 2 of Lecky, *History of European Morals*, p. 227.
44. Kolakowski, *Religion* (New York: Oxford University Press, 1982), p. 33.
45. Brinton, *A History of Western Morals* (New York: Harcourt, Brace, 1959), p. 142.

we probably can do no better than arrive at the prosaic and unspectacular conclusion that Christianity, like other human institutions, has been neither totally good nor totally bad. Both the attack on the moral record of Christianity and the assertion of its moral superiority must be regarded as polemical endeavors that cannot issue in a conclusive verdict.

It is of interest to note that while most secular humanists continue to belabor the horrors of the Inquisition in order to establish the moral depravity of Christianity, many Christian thinkers have abandoned the apologetic mode of discourse. "Christians are in no position to claim moral superiority over other men," the Protestant theologian James Gustafson has acknowledged, "or to make a case for the Christian faith on the grounds of verifiable evidence of its contribution to the moral well-being of the human community. Personal and historical evidence is not unambiguously on the Christian side."[46] Reinhold Niebuhr had earlier taken the same position.

The historical record alone can, of course, tell us nothing definitive about the moral influence of Christianity on our contemporary society, the subject of this book. The past may cast its shadow upon the present, and to the extent that Christianity is a religion that values the continuity of its doctrine, earlier traditions will continue to have an impact. Still, Christianity is also a dynamic faith, and the past therefore will not necessarily determine present-day life. It is for this reason that I have called this introductory chapter a "prologue." The real work of dealing with current realities still lies ahead.

46. Gustafson, *Christ and the Moral Life* (New York: Harper & Row, 1968), p. 239.

2. The Rise of Secularism

One of the defining characteristics of modernity is secularism, the notion that religion is a residue of intellectual backwardness and, at best, a social necessity. The idea that the uneducated masses need religion in order to be law-abiding and moral goes back to antiquity. The Greek historian of Rome, Polybius, observed that "a scrupulous fear of the Gods is the very thing which keeps the Roman common-wealth together." Since the common people are "fickle, and full of lawless desires," the only way to check the multitude is through "mysterious terrors and scenic effects of this sort."[1] The social utility of myths had been stressed by Plato and reappeared in the writings of the Stoics. "It is impossible to lead the masses of women and the common people generally to piety, holiness and faith simply by philo-sophical teaching," observed the Greek historian and geographer Strabo; "fear of God is also required, not omitting legends and miraculous stories."[2] An admirer of ancient wisdom, Machiavelli in his *Discourses* called religion "the most necessary and assured support of any civil society," and he exhorted princes and heads of republics "to uphold the foundations of the religion of their countries, for then it is easy to keep their people religious, and consequently well con-ducted and united."[3] Probably the best known of these remarks —

1. Polybius, *The Histories*, Book 6, ch. 56, trans. Evelyn S. Shuckburgh (London: Macmillan, 1889), pp. 505-6.
2. Strabo, quoted by Crane Brinton in *A History of Western Morals* (New York: Harcourt, Brace, 1959), p. 124.
3. Machiavelli, *"The Prince" and "The Discourses,"* Book 1, chs. 11 and 12 (New York: Modern Library, 1940), pp. 146, 150.

representative of the cynical and condescending views of both religion and the masses that many of these writers had — is Edward Gibbon's comment on the different modes of worship prevailing in the Roman world during the age of the Antonines: they "were all considered by the people as equally true; by the philosopher as equally false; and by the magistrate as equally useful."[4]

In the eyes of most contemporary Christian theologians, to make morality dependent upon the promise of reward for the good and punishment for the wicked is to degrade both religion and morals. And yet the crucial importance of ultimate rewards and punishments as sanctions for morality has been affirmed not only by pagans but also by many Christian thinkers throughout the centuries. John Locke wrote, "The view of heaven and hell will cast a slight upon the short pleasures and pains of this present state, and give attractions and encouragements to virtue, which reason and interest, and the care of ourselves, cannot but allow and prefer. Upon this foundation, and upon this only, morality stands firm and may defy all competition."[5]

The French philosopher Pierre Bayle, a contemporary of Locke, was one of the first modern thinkers to break with the long-held assumption of a necessary link between religion and morality. Pointing to the exemplary life led by many pagans, Bayle argued that "It is not any stranger for an atheist to live virtuously than for a Christian to commit all sorts of crimes." For most people, the real reasons for virtue were considerations of opinion and reputation and the physical sanctions of the law. Hence, as Bayle saw it, "A society of atheists would practice both civic and moral actions just as other societies practice them, provided that crimes were severely punished and that honor and shame were associated with certain acts."[6] In such a society, social order would be guaranteed not by the priest but by the hangman.

---

4. Gibbon, *The History of the Decline and Fall of the Roman Empire*, vol. 1 (London: John Murray, 1903), p. 165.

5. Locke, *The Reasonableness of Christianity*, ed. Ian Y. Ramsey (London, 1958), p. 70, cited by John Macquarrie in "Rethinking Natural Law," in *Readings in Moral Theology*, no. 2: *The Distinctiveness of Christian Ethics*, ed. Charles E. Curran and Richard A. McCormick (New York: Paulist Press, 1980), p. 132.

6. Bayle, *Pensées diverses sur les comètes* (1682), in *The Great Contest of Faith and Reason: Selections from the Writings of Pierre Bayle*, ed. Karl C. Sandburg (New York, 1963), pp. 19 and 16, cited by George A. Kelly in "Bayle's Commonwealth of Atheists Revisited," in *Religion, Morality, and the Law*, ed. Roland Pennock and John W. Chapman (New York: New York University Press, 1988), p. 94.

The Heritage of the Enlightenment

The Enlightenment of the eighteenth century manifested itself in many different ways. In England and Scotland, the Enlightenment simply continued the growing commitment to the ideas of skeptical reason and individual rights. It was in France, where these same ideas faced strong opposition, that the Enlightenment embraced far more radical claims. When speaking below of the ambivalent moral legacy of the Enlightenment, I thus mean the French Enlightenment specifically.

The French Enlightenment completed the separation of religion and morality. To be sure, many of the *philosophes* continued to believe that the common people were incapable of behaving in a moral manner without the dread sanctions of religion. Voltaire wanted (and believed in) a simple and rational religion that affirmed the existence of a God who rewarded the good and punished sinners and that reduced the power of the priesthood to a minimum. He insisted that such a religion was a necessity for all but a few philosophers and that without it society would succumb to disorder and crime. "I want my attorney, my tailor, my servants, even my wife to believe in God," he wrote in his *Philosophical Dictionary*, "and I think that then I shall be robbed and cuckolded less often."[7] But in the eyes of other leading figures of the Enlightenment, the human race had attained the ability to dispense with the props of organized religion. These thinkers believed that human beings were sovereign in their moral authority. They were naturally beneficent and sociable creatures who would find their way to the good if freed from the falsehoods taught by the corrupt priests of revealed religion. For Holbach and Diderot, convinced atheists, not only was Christianity synonymous with ignorance, superstition, and fanaticism — a view shared by most of the *philosophes* — but human society could not improve morally without repudiating belief in God altogether. One of the central goals of the French Enlightenment was to free the individual from the shackles of tradition. Since this tradition included much oppression, injustice, intolerance, and indifference to human suffering, the Enlightenment deserves credit for promoting human progress. This appraisal should be uncontroversial; it has been made by both admirers and critics of the Enlightenment. The men of

7. "A, B, C," in *Philosophical Dictionary*, vol. 2, 605, cited by Peter Gay in *The Enlightenment: An Interpretation*, vol. 2: *The Science of Freedom* (New York: Alfred A. Knopf, 1969), p. 527.

the Enlightenment, writes Peter Gay, were united in a vastly ambitious program of achieving freedom in its many forms — "freedom from arbitrary power, freedom of speech, freedom of trade, freedom to realize one's talents, freedom of aesthetic response, freedom, in a word, of moral man to make his own way in this world."[8] Or, as it was put by Lester Crocker, a far more critical historian,

> Reason, tolerance, liberty, unalienable rights, legal equality, human-itarianism, progress through enlightenment — these are imperish-able ideals which still underlie our civilization. We cannot forget that the Declaration of Independence, the Bill of Rights, and the Déclaration des Droits de l'Homme stand as immortal monuments symbolizing the legacy of the Enlightenment. In this same tradition we must add the theory of representative government and the separation of powers.[9]

But, of course, that is not the only legacy of the Enlightenment. Other less attractive characteristics of modernity are also linked to this important intellectual movement. The Enlightenment not only sought to improve humanity but also spurred the desire for perfection. The search for utopia, the endeavor to build a society that would end human conflict once and for all, in turn has been a crucial ingredient in modern totalitarianism and its horrors. Convinced that they represented the forward march of history and inevitable progress, both communist and fascist totalitarian regimes rode roughshod over all opposition and killed millions of innocent human beings who stood in their way.

Some contemporary conservative authors have seen a link between the unprecedented evils we have experienced in the twentieth century and the abandonment of God, first promoted in modern times by some of the *philosophes* of the Enlightenment. Werner Dannhauser discusses with approval Nietzsche's famous aphorism about the death of God and the consequent loss of all objective standards of right and wrong, opening the door to barbarism.[10] Stephen Tonsor, invoking

---

8. Gay, *The Enlightenment*, vol. 1: *The Rise of Modern Paganism* (New York: Alfred A. Knopf, 1966), p. 3.

9. Crocker, *Nature and Culture: Ethical Thought in the French Enlightenment* (Baltimore: Johns Hopkins University Press, 1963), p. 514.

10. Dannhauser, "The Evil of Our Time," *This World*, no. 25 (Spring 1989): 40.

Dostoyevsky, argues that "it is only after the death of God that everything will be permitted."[11]

I am not convinced by this argument — at least as concerns the
horrors perpetrated by modern totalitarianism and similar social movements. It should be noted that some of the worst offenders in the
fascist camp were Christians; hence it is difficult to regard this savagery
as caused by atheism. We know that religious zeal was an important
factor in the widespread massacres committed by the Nazi-backed
Ustasha regime in Catholic Croatia during World War II. It is estimated that 700,000 Serbs, gypsies, and Jews — men, women, and
children — were killed by the Ustasha, who tortured and mutilated
many of their victims. Religious fervor and the conviction of the
importance of fighting a crusade on behalf of religion and civilization
also explain much of the fanaticism and cruelty of Franco's forces
during the Spanish Civil War (just as hatred of religion was one of the
important causes of the excesses committed by the Republican camp).
Simone Weil was one of several Christian thinkers who have seen a
parallel between the medieval Inquisition and the enforcement of
intellectual conformity by modern totalitarian regimes.[12] Conversely,
some of the most dedicated and effective opponents of totalitarianism
have been atheists such as John Dewey and Sidney Hook. It therefore
is probably more accurate to say that modern totalitarianism is linked
to the Enlightenment primarily by its relentless drive for perfection
rather than by the rejection of God. Atheism as such was neither the
necessary nor the sufficient cause of totalitarianism.

Another negative consequence of the Enlightenment has been
modern society's lack of moral conviction. The *philosophes* denied that
Christian culture was superior to others, and they argued for the equal
worth of all kinds of institutions and forms of human conduct. This
cultural relativism was a necessary ingredient in the commendable
commitment of the Enlightenment to the cause of toleration.
"Humanist skepticism, including its dismissal of 'absolute values,'"
the philosopher Leszek Kolakowski observes, "forged a powerful
weapon against the fanaticism of sectarian strife and laid a foundation
for the institutional framework of a pluralist and tolerant society."
However, Kolakowski goes on to argue, this good seed turned out to

11. Tonsor, "Marxism and Modernity," *Modern Age*, Fall 1991, p. 8.
12. Cf. her "Sketch of Contemporary Social Life" in *The Simone Weil
Reader*, ed. George A. Panichas (New York: David McKay, 1977), p. 29.

produce dangerous fruit. "The denial of 'absolute values' for the sake of both rationalist principles and the general spirit of openness threatens our ability to make the distinction between good and evil altogether; to extend tolerance to fanaticism amounts to favoring the victory of intolerance; to abstain from fighting evil on the pretext that 'we are imperfect' might convert our imperfections into barbarity."[13] Again, however, we should not throw out the baby with the bath water. It would be wrong, as philosopher Charles Taylor has reminded us, to declare the entire Enlightenment project to be simply a mistake. Rather, "we have to avoid the error of declaring those goods invalid whose exclusive pursuit leads to contemptible or disastrous consequences."[14]

The *philosophes* of the Enlightenment hoped that human autonomous and sovereign reason would displace authority and tradition, and this idea, too, has been a mixed blessing. It is not only that reason alone cannot convince individuals to be moral. More important, the successful attack upon tradition has encouraged an extravagant individualism that recognizes no other moral standard than personal fulfillment. Freeing human beings from the constraints of inherited beliefs has led to the spread and toleration of all kinds of harmful behavior and has weakened one of the most important traditional institutions of society — the family.

The *philosophes* sought to break with traditional morality, which they regarded as a force that constrains and degrades human nature. They praised human impulses, desires, and passions, including sexuality, which they saw as an integral and laudatory part of human nature. But for some men of the Enlightenment, the onslaught against tradition and the exaltation of the natural went beyond the defense of greater sexual freedom and the repudiation of irrational sexual taboos. In his Tahitian fantasy, *Supplement au Voyage de Bougainville,* Diderot not only exalted sexual liberty but scoffed at monogamy and the fear of incest. Fornication and adultery were imaginary crimes created by religion. And from this defense of instinct over culture it was but another small step to the demented ravings of the Marquis de Sade. In a critical review of Lester Crocker's study of eighteenth-century France, Peter Gay argues that Sade was not an heir but a caricature of

13. Kolakowski, *Modernity on Endless Trial* (Chicago: University of Chicago Press, 1990), pp. 150, 152.

14. Taylor, *Sources of the Self: The Making of Modern Identity* (Cambridge, Mass.: Harvard University Press, 1989), p. 511.

the *philosophes*, but even he concedes that Sade borrowed from them.[15] Crocker is right in observing that to reduce the individual to the indiscriminately natural is indeed a sure road to nihilism.[16] We will return to this issue later in this chapter.

Secular Humanism

Sigmund Freud has been called the Enlightenment's "most distinguished representative in the twentieth century."[17] He had a secular view of human beings, and he believed that the human race will eventually outgrow the need for religion. Religion, he wrote in *The Future of an Illusion*, "is comparable to a childhood neurosis." The time will come when men and women, by withdrawing their expectations from the other world and putting all their energies into their life on earth, "will probably succeed in achieving a state of things in which life will become tolerable for everyone and civilization no longer oppressive to anyone."[18] The same conviction represents one of the core beliefs of contemporary secular humanism, another descendant of the Enlightenment.

Summary statements of the philosophy of secular humanism can be found in two manifestos issued by the humanist movement. *Humanist Manifesto I* was signed by 34 humanists in 1933, among them such well-known philosophers as John Dewey and John Herman Randall, Jr. *Humanist Manifesto II* appeared in 1973 with the endorsement of 114 prominent American intellectuals and was subsequently subscribed to by a large number of individuals from various walks of life, both in the United States and abroad. The signers included academics such as Lionel Abel, H. J. Eysenck, Herbert Feigl, Anthony Flew, Sidney Hook, and B. F. Skinner, as well as public figures such as Betty Friedan, founder of the National Organization for Women,

15. Gay, "*An Age of Crisis:* A Critical View," *Journal of Modern History* 23 (1961): 174-77. This essay is a review of Lester G. Crocker's book *An Age of Crisis: Man and World in Eighteenth-Century France* (Baltimore: Johns Hopkins University Press, 1959).

16. Crocker, *Nature and Culture*, pp. 397-98.

17. Peter Gay, *The Bridge of Criticism* (New York: Harper & Row, 1970), p. 91.

18. Freud, *The Future of an Illusion*, in *Complete Psychological Works*, vol. 21, trans. James Strachey (London: Hogarth Press, 1961), pp. 53, 50.

Alan F. Guttmacher of Planned Parenthood, and labor leader A. Philip Randolph. Neither of the two manifestos used the label "secular humanism," but the identification with secularism was nevertheless striking. Both manifestos pronounced traditional theism to be an unproved and outmoded faith. The manifesto of 1973 declared that "traditional faiths encourage dependence, rather than independence, obedience rather than affirmation, fear rather than courage," and it referred to "promises of immortal salvation or fear of eternal damnation as both illusory and harmful."[19]

In a book entitled *In Defense of Secular Humanism* (1983) and in many other publications, the philosopher Paul Kurtz defends the moral superiority of secular humanism over traditional religion. Kurtz argues that such a humanism, since it is not based on theistic illusion or obedience to an authoritarian code imposed from without, "provides man with a more secure foundation for the moral life."[20] He concedes that traditional religion can be a source of meaning and direction in life, but he claims that secular humanism can respond to these same human needs without resorting to supernatural myths and falsehoods. Common moral decencies are rooted in human nature; the development of character does not require belief in God. Humanism, he suggests, must "develop convictions based upon the best available evidence, beliefs for which we can give reasons and which yet are of sufficient force to stimulate passionate commitment."[21]

In the tradition of the Enlightenment, secular humanism affirms the central role of reason in human affairs. "Reason and Intelligence," declares *Humanist Manifesto II*, "are the most effective instruments that humankind possesses. . . . The controlled use of scientific methods, which have transformed the natural and social sciences since the Renaissance, must be extended further in the solution of human problems." Any account of nature should pass the tests of scientific evidence; "in our judgment, the dogmas and myths of traditional religions do not do so. . . . As nontheists, we begin with humans not God, nature not deity." Moral values are seen as derived from human

19. Paul Kurtz, ed., *Humanist Manifestos I and II* (Buffalo, N.Y.: Prometheus Books, 1973), p. 16.

20. Kurtz, "What Is Humanism?" in *Moral Problems in Contemporary Society: Essays in Humanistic Ethics*, ed. Paul Kurtz (Englewood Cliffs, N.J.: Prentice-Hall, 1969), p. 10.

21. Kurtz, *Eupraxophy: Living without Religion* (Buffalo, N.Y.: Prometheus Books, 1989), p. 113.

experience. "Ethics is autonomous and situational, needing no theological or ideological sanction."[22] The manifesto called for the renunciation of violence and force as methods of solving international disputes and instead proposed the creation of a world community, "a system of world law and a world order based upon transnational federal government." The world community was asked to engage in cooperative planning. "Ecological damage, resource depletion, and excessive population growth must be checked by international concord." The manifesto urged "the use of reason and compassion to produce the kind of world we want — a world in which peace, prosperity, freedom, and happiness are widely shared."[23]

Secular humanism affirms many of the permanently valuable ideals of the Enlightenment, but also shares its negative aspects. The area of personal and social morality is a case in point. It is meritorious to tolerate diversity in social arrangements, but destructive to attribute equal value to all of them. Together with some feminists and homosexuals, many secular humanists challenge the superiority of the traditional family. By considering traditional sexual norms as just one of many different bases for forming various kinds of partnerships, they give respectability to lifestyles that often have damaging social consequences.

Humanist Manifesto II decried "intolerant attitudes, often cultivated by orthodox religions and puritanical cultures, [that] unduly repress sexual conduct. . . . Without countenancing mindless permissiveness or unbridled promiscuity, a civilized society should be a tolerant one. Short of harming others or compelling them to do likewise, individuals should be permitted to express their sexual proclivities and pursue their life-styles as they desire." The manifesto called for the right to birth control, abortion, divorce, euthanasia, and suicide.[24] Much of this coincides with the basic tenets of contemporary American liberalism, though the formulation of these positions in the writings of secular humanists often carries a special edge.

Critics from the ranks of the religious right have accused secular humanists of subscribing to all kinds of immorality that threaten the moral health of the country. In his book *Listen, America!* Jerry Falwell decries secular humanists' embrace of situation ethics, which, he says,

---

22. *Humanist Manifestos I and II*, pp. 16-17.
23. Ibid., pp. 21, 23.
24. Ibid., pp. 18-19.

means "freedom from any restraint."[25] Such criticisms are often couched in somewhat shrill language, but an examination of the literature published by the secular humanist movement reveals that these denunciations are not very far off the mark. The authors of articles in *The Humanist* and *Free Inquiry* clearly speak only for themselves; there is no official secular humanist doctrine. Nevertheless, the frequency with which certain positions are voiced in these journals indicates that the editors do not consider these positions to be unacceptable. They reflect what *Humanist Manifesto II* called toleration of different lifestyles.

A frequently recurring theme is the need to re-evaluate traditional values concerning family ties and attitudes toward sex in order to free modern men and women from the encrusted moral beliefs of the past. The assumption, inherited from the Enlightenment, is that human nature is good and that it is society which distorts the individual's innocence. Thus, for example, in an article in the Winter 1970 issue of *The Humanist* entitled "Sex: In and Out of Marriage," Robert Whitehurst, a professor of sociology and anthropology, argued against the "archaic Biblical code" that prescribes the monogamous family for everyone. "It is my conviction that it *is* possible to develop more flexible sexual norms that involve pluralistic adaptations to sexuality within a humanistic framework and that will be of greater benefit to the members of society." Whether it be premarital sex or swinging, the decisive criterion, the author proposed, should be what is good for the individual, not outworn social taboos. "It will no longer suffice to attempt to use repressive norms to restrain sexuality in what by now have become relatively normal modes of expression."[26]

In its Fall 1987 issue, *Free Inquiry* published a discussion of the question "Is the sexual revolution over?" Rob Tielman, a professor of sociology at the University of Utrecht in the Netherlands and co-chairman of the International Humanist and Ethical Union, explained that if good condoms are available, "then I have no problem with teenagers being free to have intercourse. . . . Promiscuity, as such, from the humanistic point of view, is neither good nor bad. If you're talking about consenting adults, I don't see any problem with promiscuity." A second professor, Sol Gordon of Syracuse University's Institute for

---

25. Falwell, *Listen, America!* (Garden City, N.Y.: Doubleday, 1980), p. 65.
26. Whitehurst, "Sex: In and Out of Marriage," *The Humanist*, January-February 1970, pp. 27-28.

Family Research and Education, stressed that sexual freedom had to be accompanied by responsibility, but went on to say, "I'm not afraid to come out and admit that extramarital liaisons, even anonymous ones, can be important and even beneficial."[27]

Writing in the July/August 1990 issue of *The Humanist*, Marty Klein, a sex therapist from California, rejected the notion of "bad" or abnormal sex. Authentic sexuality, he claimed, has its own subjective logic and challenges social definitions of what is normal: "It challenges the role of monogamy and the nuclear family as the exclusive source of emotional comfort." Pornography, he went on to argue, has become the symbol of "bad" sex because it depicts sex without love or meaning. "But what's wrong with 'meaningless' sex if both partners agree to it? There is no reason that sex cannot or should not express our ignoble side: aggression, lust, greed, selfishness, hedonism (all with the consent of one's partner, of course)." Klein ended his essay with this advice: "Now, more than ever, it is time — emotionally and spiritually — to just say yes."[28]

Irving Kristol has criticized secular humanism for contributing to moral disarray and confusion about how to educate our children. Secular humanism, Kristol argues, fails to provide us with a moral code. "Pure reason can offer a critique of moral beliefs but it cannot engender them. . . . Pure reason cannot tell us that incest is wrong (so long as there are no offspring). . . . Pure reason cannot tell us that bestiality is wrong; indeed the only argument against bestiality these days is that, since we cannot know whether animals enjoy it or not, it is a violation of 'animal rights.'"[29]

Kristol's critique of secular humanism is not exaggerated, nor does it use inappropriate examples. The English philosopher John Harris may not be an active member of the secular humanist movement, but his denial that there is such a thing as sexual morality is perfectly in line with secular humanism's preoccupation with in-dividual self-fulfillment and gratification. According to Harris, the only sexual practices that raise legitimate moral issues are those that involve violation, injury, and/or exploitation. "I know of no evidence for the

27. "Is the Sexual Revolution Over? A *Free Inquiry* Interview with Sol Gordon and Rob Tielman," *Free Inquiry*, Fall 1987, pp. 36-37.
28. Klein, "Censorship and the Fear of Sexuality," *The Humanist*, July/August 1990, pp. 17, 38.
29. Kristol, "The Future of American Jewry," *Commentary*, August 1991, p. 25.

harmful effects of bestiality, but any that there may be would have to be worse than depriving animal lovers of sexual release. . . ." The same holds true for necrophilia (sexual intercourse with a dead body), as long as the dead person has agreed to this in advance, and for fetishism, incest, and sodomy. As Harris sees it, the fact that we regard such behavior as obscene or disgusting "is no evidence at all for its immorality."[30] Bertrand Russell, a self-avowed atheist, built upon the same premises when he called opposition to adultery irrational. "Moral rules ought not to be such as to make instinctive happiness impossible. Yet that is the effect of strict monogamy, in a community where the number of the two sexes are very unequal."[31]

Not surprisingly, the same single-minded pursuit of self-interest leads secular humanists to endorse the morality of abortion. Humanists, argued a contributor to *Free Inquiry* in 1989, should defend not only freedom of choice but "the moral acceptability of abortion per se." A woman's right to terminate a pregnancy should be absolute. The right of the state in certain situations to protect potential life, established in *Roe v. Wade*, represents a limitation of individual liberty "that civil libertarians should justly find frightening."[32] Writing in a 1989 issue of *The Humanist*, a physician-director of an abortion clinic in Boulder, Colorado, celebrated abortion as the most dramatic example of the new freedom of women to choose not to reproduce: "It is the final and irretrievable act of fertility control a woman can exercise in a particular pregnancy."[33] There is no recognition here that abortion takes the life of a developing human being. It can be argued that in certain very exceptional circumstances it may be morally acceptable to terminate a pregnancy. But surely such an act, like all instances of killing, requires a special justification and should not be regarded as morally right per se.

That same pursuit of self-interest drives some women to defend prostitution as just another kind of work — "sex work" is the politically correct term. According to Priscilla Alexander, co-director of COYOTE (the acronym for "Call Off Your Old Tired Ethics") and author of *Sex Work* (1987), the important thing is that women have the right to

30. Harris, *The Value of Life* (London: Routledge & Kegan Paul, 1985), pp. 176-77.

31. Russell, *What I Believe* (New York: E. P. Dutton, 1925), p. 50.

32. Tom Flynn, "The Future of Abortion," *Free Inquiry*, Fall 1989, p. 44.

33. Warren M. Hern, "Abortion as Insurrection," *The Humanist*, March/April 1989, p. 18.

determine for themselves how they will use their own bodies. Similar sentiments can be found in a more recent anthology, Gail Pheterson's *A Vindication of the Rights of Whores* (1989).[34] Again, these women may or may not consider themselves secular humanists. However, there can be no doubt that the exaltation of self-fulfillment and individual freedom, no matter what the consequences for the moral quality of society, conforms indeed to the very essence of secular humanism.

In this kind of cultural milieu, even the consumption of drugs is considered a matter of individual choice. The September/October 1990 issue of *The Humanist* included six articles against the war on drugs. One of the arguments, pressed by a psychopharmacologist, was that the use of drugs is a "natural part of our biology. . . . In a sense, the war on drugs is a war against ourselves, a denial of our very nature."[35]

Very occasionally a humanist author will voice some mildly worded disagreements with the movement's dedication to individual fulfillment. In an article entitled "Sexual Morality for Young Humanists and Their Parents," Devin Carroll pointed out that a great deal of sexual behavior in today's society involves potentially harmful consequences and is characterized by lack of responsibility, and therefore should be considered immoral. But this criticism did not reach very far. Thus, for example, Carroll saw no moral problem with practices such as open marriages, though he termed them "unwise."[36] As this and the preceding examples show, the vast majority of the articles in the journals of the secular humanist movement expound the superiority of self-gratification and accept the motto "If it feels good, do it." Such counsel not only runs counter to the most basic values of our culture but is by now rejected as psychologically damaging by many clinicians.

Many mental-health practitioners share secular humanists' preoccupation with selfish and hedonistic values and do not acknowledge that behavior motivated by these values can be highly destructive to both mental health and societal integrity. "The pleasure principle," notes William Kilpatrick, "is not a very good rule for social order. Sooner or later, sexual irresponsibility, adulteries, diseases, neglected

34. Cf. the discussion by Mark Satin in "Some of Our Daughters, Some of Our Lovers," *New Options*, no. 71 (October/November 1990): 3.

35. Ronald K. Siegel, "Intoxication: The 'Fourth Drive,'" *The Humanist*, September/October 1990, p. 27.

36. Carroll, "Sexual Morality for Young Humanists and Their Parents," *The Humanist*, July/August 1989, pp. 41, 44.

children and abandoned families become everyone's problem."[37] Addressing this state of affairs, Donald Campbell, in his presidential address to the American Psychological Association in 1975, criticized the secularist and hedonistic values widely prevalent among psychologists. Modern psychology and psychiatry in all their major forms, he declared, "are more hostile to the inhibitory messages of traditional religious moralizing than is scientifically justified." All the major religions, Campbell pointed out, have taught that human traits such as greed, lust, and selfishness should be curbed, while psychology and psychiatry "not only describe man as selfishly motivated, but implicitly and explicitly teach that he ought to be so." The repression of individual impulses is seen as undesirable; guilt is seen as "a dysfunctional neurotic blight." Campbell concluded with a warning against the "epistemic arrogance of behavioral and social scientists," and he recommended "respect for the wisdom that well-winnowed traditions may contain about how life should be lived."[38]

Another recurring theme in the literature of secular humanism is the harsh assault upon traditional religion, especially Christianity. Some attacks take the form of questioning the historicity of events such as the Resurrection or casting doubt upon the possibility of miracles. More often, one finds articles written by polemicists such as Avro Manhattan, Paul Blanshard, and others of lesser renown who ridicule and disdain the Christian faith.

In an article typical of this kind of writing, James Jarrett, a professor of philosophy, argued that humanism must oppose superstition, metaphysical speculation, and the "puerile ethics of traditional religion." Throughout history, he maintained, the churches have promulgated "cruelty and violence"; they divert "energy from ethics to ritual and ceremonial observance of rules."[39] The Bible, wrote another humanist, praises slavery and theocracy. The Bible-god is pleased "to save those who believe the moronic message Paul peddles."[40] According

37. Kilpatrick, *Why Johnny Can't Tell Right from Wrong* (New York: Simon & Schuster, 1992), p. 69.

38. Campbell, "On the Conflicts between Biological and Social Evolution and between Psychology and Moral Tradition," *American Psychologist* 30 (1975): 1103-4, 1120-21.

39. Jarrett, "Must Religious Humanism Be Thin?" *The Humanist* 10 (1950): 108.

40. Delos B. McKnown, "Humanism, Disbelief, and Bibliolatry," *The Humanist*, May/June 1990, pp. 8-9.

to a feminist contributor, free thought and feminism are inseparable. How, she asked, "can you be a feminist if you refuse to defer to men on Earth but submit to a divine authority? . . . Jesus offered 'pie in the sky' egalitarianism for souls in heaven but not on earth, never condemning servitude or slavery."[41] Alcohol, drugs, and tobacco also provide comfort and solace to people, argued Isaac Asimov, then president of the American Humanist Association, in an article published in 1989. "Judge by solace and comfort only and there is no behavior we ought to interfere with." The world is threatened by overpopulation, pollution, the greenhouse effect, and the danger of nuclear war. "If our only answer to all this is a superstitious reliance on something outside ourselves as a solution to all those problems, we are making that destruction certain."[42] While a few humanists concede that religious teachers such as Jesus provided an example of how to lead an upstanding moral life, the writings of most humanists seek to discredit Christianity and brand it a self-deception and delusion. Prometheus Books, a publishing house headed by the secular humanist philosopher Paul Kurtz, publishes titles such as *The Forgery of the Old Testament* and *The Final Superstition: A Critical Evaluation of the Judeo-Christian Legacy.* In the same spirit of libertinism, Prometheus also features books about sadomasochism, the "next sexual revolution," as well as guides to sexually explicit materials. The *X-Rated Videotape Star Index 1994,* according to Prometheus's Fall-Winter 1994-1995 catalogue, "features 17,000 porno movies," and enables the reader to find his or her "favorite stars at their tantalizing best. . . . Some stars are featured with quick biographical data or physical descriptions." The book is described as the most complete index of adult entertainment ever. "What more could you want?" the publisher asks.

There exists a Fellowship of Religious Humanists, organized in 1963, that does not share the anti-religious sentiments of secular humanists. Writing in the fellowship's magazine *Religious Humanism,* one Walter Bernard criticized the failure of all humanists to "satisfy the spiritual need that was created when theism and organized religion were abandoned by them." To fill this void they emphasize social and political activism, but, he argued, human beings cannot feel at home

---

41. Annie Laurie Gaylor, "Feminist 'Salvation,'" *The Humanist,* July/August 1988, p. 33.

42. Asimov, "The Never-ending Fight," *The Humanist,* March/April 1989, pp. 7-8.

in such a cold universe. Secular humanists in particular, Bernard maintained, completely ignore or deprecate the spiritual side of individuals: "They want man to be satisfied with materialism and with science based on it and ignore man's yearning for a positive relationship to the totality of Being."[43]

A related observation was made by the philosopher Marvin Kohl, a signer of *Humanist Manifesto II*. In an article in *Free Inquiry*, Kohl noted that the fact that there exist many millions of devout believers may indicate that belief in God — or at least in the idea that the cosmos is guided by a loving purpose — may fulfill some basic human need. It is possible that belief in God produces at least as great a proportion of good over evil as does any other available known alternative. Hence "to arrogantly crusade against religious belief — without distinguishing between beneficent and nonbeneficent varieties — may very well diminish important elements of human welfare."[44] Also writing in *Free Inquiry* and drawing on his research on religion and crime, the sociologist William Bainbridge pointed out that secularization is not an unmixed blessing and "is associated with a weakening of the moral and social fabric of society as well. The death of religion would introduce not a happy age of scientific enlightenment but an age of severely aggravated social problems, of which suicide and crime are but two examples."[45] Both of these articles were published in 1981. There is no indication that these kinds of arguments have had any effect on the thinking of secular humanists.

The "Secular Humanist Declaration," publicized in the first issue of *Free Inquiry* in 1980, called for the cultivation of moral development in children and young adults, but warned against the danger of an "absolutist morality." Secular humanism, the declaration explained, is "not so much a specific morality as it is a method for the explanation and discovery of moral principles."[46] This way of approaching the task of moral education is in line with what educationists call "values clarification," a teaching technique that fits in well with secular humanism's stress on relativism.

43. Bernard, "Reflections on the Basic Idea of Religious Humanism," *Religious Humanism* 10 (1976): 2, 7.

44. Kohl, "The Meaning of Life and Belief in God," *Free Inquiry*, Spring 1981, p. 35.

45. Bainbridge, "Comment on Daniel Bell's 'The Return of the Sacred,'" *Free Inquiry*, Fall 1981, p. 29.

46. "A Secular Humanist Declaration," *Free Inquiry*, Winter 1980/81, p. 5.

Values clarification is an outgrowth of curriculum projects of the 1960s that opposed the teaching of facts and instead stressed the importance of knowing how to think. Its earliest proponent was an educator at Ohio State University and New York University, Louis Raths, who, together with two co-authors, published a book entitled *Values and Teaching* in 1966. Influenced by John Dewey, Raths rejected the idea of universally valid rules of conduct and traditional modes of moral education, which he branded indoctrination. Instead, Raths proposed teaching children how to make informed choices. The emphasis was to be on the process of valuing, not on the results. Teachers, through questioning, would help students acquire the skills of developing well-thought-out moral positions; they would not judge responses as better or worse. As a result, Raths suggested, there would be less confusion, apathy, and inconsistency. Values clarification would enhance rationality, thoughtfulness, and respect for others.[47]

By 1972, about 2,000 educators had been reached through workshops on values clarification, and from that point on the technique spread rapidly. With its stress on process rather than substantive moral judgment, values clarification harmonized with the spirit of skepticism and alienation then rampant in the country. But there was also criticism. Values clarification, Alan Lockwood argued, communicated the view that all values are equally valid. The moral choices of Adolf Hitler and Albert Schweitzer were equally acceptable and praiseworthy as long as they conformed to the prescribed process of deliberation.[48] Another critic pointed out the similarity of values clarification to Carl Rogers' client-centered therapy. Both techniques were based on the relativistic view that what matters is not whether what one believes is true or justified but whether it is sincere and genuine. Values clarification represented a betrayal of reason and a retreat into irrationalism. "How else can one characterize the unconditional acceptance of the child as the ultimate source of appeal for what is true, right or justified?"[49] In her book entitled *Democratic Education*, Amy Gutman suggested that

---

47. Raths et al., *Values and Teaching: Working with Values in the Classroom*, 2nd ed. (Columbus, Ohio: Charles E. Merrill, 1978), pp. 4-5, 289-90. See also Howard Kirschenbaum, *Advanced Value Clarification* (La Jolla, Calif.: University Associates, 1977).

48. Lockwood, "A Critical View of Values Clarification," *Teachers College Record* 78 (1975): 46.

49. A. C. Kazepides, "The Logic of Value Clarification," *Journal of Educational Thought* 11 (1977): 103-4.

by treating every moral opinion as equally worthy, values clarification "encourages children in the false subjectivism that 'I have my opinion and you have yours and who's to say who's right?'" Children who believe in the inferiority of blacks, she maintained, need criticism, not just a clarification of their values.[50]

Values clarification has an obvious appeal to secular humanists, who, like the advocates of values clarification, consider all questions of morality to be open and resolvable through reason. The possibility that many young people today suffer not from a defect in reasoning but from a defect in character is not considered. When criticized, both groups insist that they are not committed to any particular moral position and merely want to see to it that all beliefs receive a fair hearing. But this alleged neutrality is a myth. As William Bennett has correctly pointed out, the emphasis on "questioning" and "critiquing" traditional values rather than nurturing them is itself a means of advancing the agenda of modernist, secular ethics.[51] "Although ostensibly 'neutral' with regard to values," writes James Hitchcock, "this technique in fact undermines values children have learned from their parents or from the church."[52]

As a social or political movement, humanism in America is numerically weak and insignificant. In 1988, one of its leading figures, Paul Kurtz, estimated the total membership of all humanist organizations to be no more than 12,000. This figure included the approximately 3,200 members of the twenty Ethical Culture Societies as well as the members of the Fellowship of Religious Humanists, many of whom are not *secular* humanists. On the other hand, some of the members of the Unitarian Universalist Association, an organization that considers itself a church and enjoys a religious tax exemption, are secular humanists by persuasion. In an article published in 1985, the Unitarian minister Robert Eddy declared, "I am a member of a Unitarian Universalist Church and proud of it. My religion is secular humanism."[53] We do not know how many other members of the

50. Gutman, *Democratic Education* (Princeton, N.J.: Princeton University Press, 1987), p. 56.

51. Bennett, "Getting Ethics," *Commentary*, December 1980, p. 64.

52. Hitchcock, *What Is Secular Humanism? Why Humanism Became Secular and How It Is Changing Our World* (Ann Arbor, Mich.: Servant Books, 1982), p. 108.

53. Eddy, "Humanism: Secular and Religious," *Religious Humanism* 19 (1985): 32.

Unitarian Universalist Association similarly consider themselves secular humanists, but even if all of them did, we are dealing with a rather small group. In 1989 the Unitarian Universalist Association had 177,000 members nationwide. This represents about .01 percent of all Americans belonging to a religious body.[54]

Although secular humanism as an organized movement has relatively few members, the secular humanist mind-set nevertheless has an influence upon modern culture that is extensive and far-reaching. There is no need to posit the existence of an organized conspiracy in order to recognize that secular humanism represents a body of ideas with a substantial following among what has been termed the knowledge class — academics, professionals, members of the media (e.g., journalists and celebrities) — in particular. If we look at the ideology governing the intellectual elites of today's society, we cannot but conclude that secularism and modernity have become essentially synonymous. Among these groups, indifference to traditional religion and its values is pronounced. For some time now this secularist outlook has been spreading into the larger society because it reflects new social experiences such as industrialization and life in anonymous urban centers. In many ways, therefore, secular humanism is as much effect as it is cause.

Popular culture is a good barometer of this trend, which gathered strength during the 1960s. New, more permissive attitudes toward sexuality in particular were part of the cultural revolution that overtook the nation during those years of disillusionment and rebellion. While the country as a whole has since returned to a more stable pattern of life and has even experienced a wave of what some call "new traditionalism," popular culture never fully recovered from the shock waves of the 1960s and its attendant cultural attitudes. Expressive individualism, characterized by the desire for self-gratification and the display of moral recklessness, today is rampant in popular music and other forms of entertainment. The movies and television in particular flaunt the new persuasion of radical individualism, a disdain for traditional values and institutions, and the espousal of recreational promiscuity without personal commitment. "Illegitimacy chic," the movie critic Michael Medved has observed, "is as much part of the contemporary Hollywood scene as a passion for distributing condoms or saving the rain forests." An impressive array of prominent stars proudly bear children without the benefit

54. U.S. Bureau of the Census, *Statistical Abstract of the United States 1991* (Washington, D.C.: Government Printing Office, 1991), Table 78, p. 57.

of matrimony, and the same arrangement is celebrated in many of the films and television programs in which they perform.[55] Sometimes concern is expressed about birth control or sexually transmitted diseases — but not with any consistency. The message sent to teenagers watching these programs is that people can indulge in sex without worrying about consequences; Planned Parenthood speaks of massive sex *disinformation*.[56]

We cannot assess with any accuracy the impact of popular culture upon the lives of the people of this country, but we do know that the stars of the entertainment world have always served as role models. Young people in particular emulate featured performers and celebrities in manner and style. It would be simplistic to explain the increase in single-parent families and out-of-wedlock births exclusively in terms of the influence of popular culture or any other set of ideas. At the same time, it probably is only fair to note that the entertainment industry and the knowledge classes generally, imbued with a highly individualistic and secularist outlook on life, are less than helpful in reversing the crisis of the traditional family. If the nation's media and popular entertainers were to stress the importance of hard work and responsibility, the efforts of parents to teach their children the values of self-reliance and accountability would be greatly strengthened. But we are facing a different scenario. Bolstered by popular culture, the modernist ethic of sensual gratification has weakened the value of self-restraint. The toleration of different lifestyles has called into question the essential value of the monogamous family. Ideas have consequences.

55. For additional details, see Michael Medved's "Hollywood Chic: Illegitimacy and Hypocrisy," *Washington Post*, 4 October 1992.

56. These findings are discussed by David G. Myers in *The Pursuit of Happiness: Who Is Happy — and Why* (New York: William Morrow, 1992), p. 164.

3. *The Culture of Modernity and Its Social Consequences*

Many of the severe social problems experienced by the United States and other contemporary Western societies are caused, or at least aggravated, by the spread of secularism and the weakening of traditional values such as self-restraint, responsibility, and accountability. As I will try to demonstrate in this chapter, the crisis of the family and the growth of an urban underclass in particular are clearly linked to the cultural revolution that the modern world has experienced during the last thirty years.

The Decline of the Family

The symptoms of family decline are manifold and striking. The number of cohabiting unmarried couples in the United States tripled during the 1970s and nearly doubled again during the 1980s.[1] In today's society, divorce is available upon request and carries no social stigma. The religious and moral bonds that hold families together have been loosened as more and more people think of themselves as rights-bearing and pleasure-seeking individuals who form and sever relationships with other people according to their own convenience.[2] In the United States in 1970, there were 47 divorced persons for every 1,000 married persons; by 1989 there were 138.[3] Between 1970 and 1992, the pro-

---

1. U.S. Bureau of the Census, *Statistical Abstract of the United States: 1991* (Washington, D.C.: Government Printing Office, 1991), Table 53, p. 44.
2. Cf. Phillip E. Johnson, "The ACLU Philosophy and the Right to Abuse the Unborn," *Criminal Justice Ethics*, Winter/Spring 1990, p. 50.
3. *Statistical Abstract of the United States: 1991*, Tables 51, 70, 1440, pp. 43, 53, 838.

portion of children under eighteen living with only a mother increased from 11 percent to 23 percent. The percentage of children born to unmarried women jumped from 11 to 28 percent between 1970 and 1990.[4] In the face of these figures, one cannot but conclude that the traditional family is in a state of serious crisis.

The consequences of family disruption are especially serious for children. There is general agreement among social scientists that in today's society family structure has become the most important determinant of children's well-being, more important than race, geography, or any other factor. Babies born to unmarried mothers have a far higher rate of mortality. Families headed by a single mother have a poverty rate of 55 percent, five times as high as the poverty rate among two-parent families. In the nation's inner cities, poverty is overwhelmingly related to marital status. Since 1965, single mothers and their children have constituted the fastest-growing segment of the poor. Such children are more likely to have psychological and behavioral problems in and out of school, and their rate of achievement will be drastically lower.[5]

By now there exists an impressive body of research that supports the superiority of the traditional family over all rival arrangements. All attempts to ignore certain givens of human nature — as in some Israeli kibbutzim and the communes of the 1960s and early 1970s in this country — have ended in failure. The question is not whether the contemporary form of the family is God-given or the only natural one. Nor do defenders of the traditional family ignore the problems that have arisen. In the words of Brigitte and Peter Berger, who have called for a concerted defense of the family,

> We are not blind to the tensions and dissatisfactions of the bourgeois family. We are conscious of its sociohistorical relativity, and we do not wish to absolutize it in an ideologically conservative manner. However, we believe that there is no viable alternative to the bourgeois family for the raising of children who will have a good chance of becoming responsible and autonomous individuals, nor do we see

4. *Statistical Abstract of the United States: 1993*, Tables 80 and 101, pp. 64 and 78.

5. For a good discussion of the numerous studies of this subject, see Daniel Patrick Moynihan's "The Underclass: Toward a Post-Industrial Social Policy," *Public Interest*, no. 96 (Summer 1989): 16-27, and, more recently, Sara McLanahan's and Gary Sandefur's *Growing Up with a Single Parent: What Hurts, What Helps* (Cambridge, Mass.: Harvard University Press, 1994).

alternative arrangements by which adults, from youth to old age, will be given a stable context for the affirmation of themselves and their values. The defense of the bourgeois family, therefore, is not an exercise in romantic nostalgia. It is something to be undertaken in defense of human happiness and human dignity in a difficult time.[6]

No direct causal relationship has been established between female-headed households and delinquency. However, we do know that the absence of an effective father impedes the ability of a child to learn to control aggression and that children growing up in families lacking the bond of affection and consistent discipline are more likely to become delinquent. There also is evidence that many people in the impoverished inner cities experience so much stress that their child-rearing practices suffer badly. Additionally, people unable to raise law-abiding children appear to lack the cognitive and/or temperamental traits that would enable them to find and hold good jobs and secure and maintain decent housing. Children raised in these kinds of homes will be at a higher risk of delinquency, and this risk increases sharply when the mother in a mother-only household is also a teenager.[7]

Violence committed by young people has been rising at an alarming rate. According to FBI statistics, between 1968 and 1988 there was a 53 percent increase in murder, rape, robbery, and assault carried out by males and females under the age of seventeen. Between 1984 and 1993, the number of homicides among juveniles involving handguns increased fivefold. In the nation's capital between 1990 and 1992, the number of teenage girls arrested for assault and other violent crimes increased by 57 percent.[8] There is a growing consensus that these sharp increases in youth violence reflect the failure of many families to socialize their children properly. When children fail to learn self-control during their early years, they may exhibit a wide spectrum of antisocial behaviors in later life. Such poorly socialized children are more vulnerable to drugs, violence on television, and the easy avail-

6. Berger and Berger, *The War over the Family: Capturing the Middle Ground* (Garden City, N.Y.: Doubleday, 1983), p. 167.

7. James Q. Wilson, "Strategic Opportunities for Delinquency Prevention," in *Families, Schools, and Delinquency Prevention*, ed. James Q. Wilson and Glenn C. Loury (New York: Springer, 1987), p. 294.

8. Nancy Lewis, "Delinquent Girls Take a Violent Turn," *Washington Post,* 23 December 1992. See also "As Cities Reach Record Numbers of Killings, Youths Play Grim Role," *New York Times,* 1 January 1994; Fox Butterfield, "Grim Forecast Is Offered on Rising Juvenile Crime," *New York Times,* 8 September 1995.

ability of guns.[9] Clearly, to support the institution of marriage is to do more than to endorse a particular lifestyle. To ignore the importance of stable families, especially families able to raise their offspring in a proper manner, is to ignore the most crucial factor that determines the well-being of our children.

The decline of the family is the result of many factors. Some of them are mainly structural and demographic, such as the disappearance of the family as a unit of production and the movement of women into the labor force. Other factors represent broad cultural shifts. There has been a weakening of religious stigmatization of unconventional behavior. Traditional values such as commitment, fidelity, and sacrifice for the sake of others have lost importance. Instead, we find a new stress on personal autonomy, self-expression, and sexual freedom. The sense of responsibility toward even close family members has become subordinated to the overriding value of self-realization. Again, we encounter the triumph of radical individualism, the governing ethos of modernity, as the appropriate summary description of these many different changes in attitudes and values.

All of these trends have intensified during the past thirty years. The moral norm that a man should marry a woman he has made pregnant has weakened because of the greater ability of women to support themselves and the easy availability of abortion. The sexual revolution in particular has been a major contributor to the sharp increase in unwed parenthood in this country. Teenagers today are bombarded with sexually explicit messages in songs, videos, and movies. Sexual fulfillment is part of the search for immediate gratification that has become so important to today's "me generation." The percentage of Americans who condemned premarital sex as wrong declined from 68 percent in 1969 to 39 percent in 1985. Between 1971 and 1982, the proportion of unmarried girls between the ages of fifteen and nineteen who engaged in sexual intercourse jumped from 28 to 44 percent.[10] The ability of parents

---

9. Cf. Fox Butterfield, "Seeds of Murder Epidemic: Teen-age Boys with Guns," *New York Times,* 9 October 1992; see also the figures given by Thomas Lickona in *Educating for Character: How Our Schools Can Teach Respect and Responsibility* (New York: Bantam Books, 1992), p. 4.

10. Dennis K. Orthner, "The Family in Transition," in *Rebuilding the Nest: A New Commitment to the American Family,* ed. David Blankenhorn et al. (Milwaukee: Family Service America, 1990), p. 103; David Popenoe, *Disturbing the Nest: Family Change and Decline in Modern Societies* (New York: Aldine de Gruyter, 1988), p. 41.

TABLE 3.1
Births to Unmarried Women as Percent of All Births

	Whites	Blacks
1970	6%	38%
1980	11	55
1990	20	65
1992	23	68

Source: *Statistical Abstract of the United States: 1995*, Table 94, p. 77.

to counter these libertarian trends has been weakened by schools that distribute condoms against the expressed wishes of parents and by court decisions allowing abortions without parental permission.

The crisis of the family today is especially acute in the African-American community. As can be seen from Table 3.1, the percentage of births to unwed mothers, one of the most important indicators of family erosion, is substantially greater among blacks than among whites, and greatest of all among blacks without a high-school diploma. This fact helps explain why blacks, although only 12 percent of the population, make up more than half of what is known as the underclass — defined as inhabitants of the inner cities who not only suffer from poverty but also are dependent on welfare; as a group, they also have a large number of female-headed households with children.[11] Today, 41 percent of black women have a child by the time they are twenty, and nine out of ten births to black teens are out of wedlock. In 1986, Joyce Ladner, a professor of social work at Howard University, wrote an essay in which she identified teenage pregnancy as the problem most threatening to future generations of the African-American community.[12] In 1990, Georgia McMurray, another expert, noted that the incidence of pregnancy and parenting among black youths "is pervasive enough to threaten the quality of life in many poor communities and maybe even the very survival of family life as it has now evolved among Americans of African descent."[13]

11. Christopher Jencks, "Is the American Underclass Growing?" in *The Urban Underclass*, ed. Christopher Jencks and Paul E. Peterson (Washington, D.C.: Brookings Institution, 1991), pp. 88-89.

12. Ladner, "Teenage Pregnancy: The Implications for Black America," in *The State of Black America 1986*, ed. James D. Williams (New York: National Urban League, 1986), p. 65.

13. McMurray, "Those of Broader Vision: An African-American Perspective

TABLE 3.2
**Female-headed (Single, Never Married) Families
as Percent of All Families**

	Whites	Blacks
1980	11%	27%
1994	18	43

Source: *Statistical Abstract of the United States: 1995*, Table 75, p. 63.

The increase in the proportion of out-of-wedlock births in America is in part the result of a sharp decrease in the number of children born to married women. On the other hand, given the increase in premarital sexual activity among all groups of the population, the number of children born out of wedlock would have been still larger had it not been for the increased resort to abortions, which more than doubled during the period examined. Whatever the overall trends, the fact remains that today about two-thirds of all black babies are born out of wedlock, a ratio significantly higher than that among the white population, and the disparity remains after we control for age, education, and economic status.[14] The rise in the number of out-of-wedlock births in the Afro-American community, in turn, has been an important cause of the sharp increase in the number of female-headed black families (see Table 3.2), a major source of the persistently large gap between family incomes of blacks and whites. By 1994, 60 percent of all black children were living in female-headed families; for whites, the corresponding figure was 21 percent.[15] Among poor blacks in inner cities, single-parent families have come to outnumber married-couple families by more than three to one.

One of the first social scientists to draw attention to the crisis of the black family was the noted black sociologist Franklin Frazier. In an article published in 1950, he wrote,

> As the result of family disorganization a large proportion of Negro children and youth have not undergone the socialization which only the family can provide. The disorganized families have failed to

on Teenage Pregnancy and Parenting," in *The State of Black America 1990*, ed. Janet Dewart (New York: National Urban League, 1990), p. 195.

14. James Q. Wilson, "A New Approach to Welfare Reform: Humility," *Wall Street Journal*, 29 December 1994.

15. *Statistical Abstract of the United States: 1995*, Table 71, p. 61.

provide for their emotional needs and have not provided the discipline and habits which are necessary for personality development.

Family disorganization, Frazier argued, "has been partially responsible for a large amount of juvenile delinquency and adult crime among Negroes."[16]

Fifteen years later, in 1965, Daniel Patrick Moynihan, who was then Assistant Secretary of Labor in the Johnson administration, pointed to the instability of the black family as a major cause of poverty and welfare dependency among blacks. Nearly a quarter of all black births, Moynihan observed, were out of wedlock; almost one fourth of all black families were headed by females. "At the heart of the deterioration of Negro society is the deterioration of the Negro family. It is the fundamental source of the weakness of the Negro community at the present time." Unless the damage to the black family was repaired, Moynihan concluded, "all the effort to end discrimination and poverty and injustice will come to little."[17]

Moynihan's report, an internal document, was leaked and created a storm of controversy. The latter part of the 1960s was the beginning of the era of black pride. In the eyes of his critics, Moynihan had blamed the victim instead of addressing the true causes of black poverty such as lack of opportunity and racial discrimination. For many years to come, the tribulations of the black family were a taboo subject. Some of those who did tackle the subject of the black family argued that black families were strong and able to adjust to the hardships caused by discrimination and poverty. Others, while conceding the existence of a problem, attributed it to structural factors. In a much-discussed book, *The Black Family in Slavery and Freedom: 1750-1925* (1976), the historian Herbert Gutman demonstrated convincingly that the black family had not crumbled under the impact of slavery. But going beyond this solidly supported finding, Gutman then expressed ideologically fashionable views. The recently observed increase in family breakups, he argued, was due to unemployment and other difficulties blacks had experienced in the northern cities to

16. Frazier, "Problems and Needs of Negro Children and Youth Resulting from Family Disorganization," *Journal of Negro Education*, Summer 1950, pp. 276-77, quoted in Lee Rainwater and William L. Yancey's *The Moynihan Report and the Politics of Controversy* (Cambridge, Mass.: MIT Press, 1967), p. 94.

17. Moynihan, "The Negro Family: The Case for Action," in ibid., pp. 54-55, 51.

which they had migrated. Gutman, too, warned against blaming the victim.[18]

Meanwhile, rates of out-of-wedlock births and other indices of family erosion continued to rise among blacks — in good times as well as bad. The trend did not correlate with the unemployment rate or similar social indicators. In 1984, Charles Murray advanced a new explanation for the rapid rise in black single families. In his book entitled *Losing Ground: American Social Policy, 1950-1981*, he argued that welfare payments actually encouraged family breakup. Since most of the states did not provide AFDC benefits (Aid to Families with Dependent Children) when fathers lived at home, welfare assistance in effect provided an incentive for men to beget children without assuming responsibility for supporting them. But this explanation was not fully convincing, either. Critics acknowledged that increases in welfare benefits accounted for a modest increase in the proportion of female-headed families, but they asserted that welfare assistance could explain neither the magnitude of the trend nor the fact that the problem was so much more severe in the black community than in the white community. It turned out that the number of single-parent families increased even when the value of AFDC benefits in real dollars declined. It would be mindless, Moynihan conceded in 1985, to say that welfare had no effect on the incidence of welfare dependency. However, he concluded, "family deterioration neither proceeds nor responds to efforts at relief."[19] This view is shared today by most students of the subject, regardless of political persuasion.[20]

What, then, does account for the crisis of the black family? The honest answer is that we do not really know. As with all large-scale social changes, no single factor appears able to explain the trend. Most likely, we are dealing with a number of mutually reinforcing causes: economic and other conditions that make it difficult for young, male African-Americans to find jobs, social policies that encourage welfare

18. Gutman, *The Black Family in Slavery and Freedom: 1750-1925* (New York: Pantheon, 1976), p. 468.

19. Moynihan, *Family and Nation* (New York: Harcourt Brace Jovanovich, 1986), p. 158. See also Robert Moffitt, "The Effect of the U.S. Welfare System on Marital Status," *Journal of Public Economics* 41 (1990): 101-24.

20. Cf. James Q. Wilson, "The Rediscovery of Character: Private Virtue and Public Policy," *Public Interest*, no. 81 (Fall 1985): 8. See also Charles Murray, "Does Welfare Bring More Babies?" *American Enterprise*, January/February 1994, pp. 52-59.

dependency, the inferior education received by blacks, and, most importantly, changes in the values and attitudes of inner-city youths. These changes, in turn, appear to result from new societal norms such as weakened kinship ties, greater sexual permissiveness, and the erosion of traditional values. For reasons that we do not fully understand, inner-city black youths have been more strongly affected by these currents of modernity.

Inner-city ghettos, it appears, manifest a greater tolerance of deviant behavior. In his 1965 study *Dark Ghetto*, the psychologist Kenneth Clark noted that "in the ghetto, the meaning of the illegitimate child is not ultimate disgrace. There is not the demand for abortion or for surrender of the child that one finds in more privileged communities."[21] Similarly, a 1979 survey of black teenage girls in Chicago found little aversion to unwed pregnancy. Another author reported that people in the inner city show pride in all their kin, especially new babies.[22] Elijah Anderson, an astute observer, has described the "fast" adolescent street culture that regards early sexual experience and promiscuity as virtues. For the inner-city girl, pregnancy often brings dreams of marriage and the hope of a stable future:

> For many such girls who have few other perceivable options, motherhood, accidental or otherwise, becomes a rite of passage to adulthood. Although an overwhelming number may not be actively trying to have babies, many are not actively trying to prevent it. . . . With the dream of a mate, a girl may be indifferent to the possibility of pregnancy, even if it is not likely that pregnancy will lead to marriage.[23]

For boys, sexual conquests are a matter of pride and status in their peer group. "For many, the object is to hit and run while maintaining personal freedom and independence from conjugal ties. . . . Concerned with immediate gratification, some boys want babies to demonstrate their ability to control a girl's mind and body."[24] Black young men in

21. Clark, *Dark Ghetto* (New York: Harper & Row, 1965), p. 72.

22. The two surveys are discussed by Glenn C. Loury in his valuable essay "The Family as Context for Delinquency Prevention: Demographic Trends and Political Realities," in *Families, Schools, and Delinquency Prevention*, ed. Wilson and Loury, p. 16.

23. Anderson, "Neighborhood Effects on Teenage Pregnancy," in *The Urban Underclass*, ed. Jencks and Peterson, p. 383.

24. Ibid.

their teens, who were interviewed by Bill Moyers for a television program, voiced pride in their virility and for having fathered several babies. The task of drawing the young black male of our inner cities into the role of husband and father — a critical task for any civilized society — clearly is not succeeding today. "Human progress depends decisively on the socialization of the male," James Q. Wilson has written, "[but] for biological and evolutionary reasons this socialization is not easily achieved, and some substantial part of what is called the underclass problem arises from the incomplete — and increasingly more difficult — task of socializing some males."[25]

The years after the Moynihan report of 1965 saw the emergence of "black sociology." As many black social scientists and other black writers saw it, what to white, middle-class observers appeared to be instability was simply natural adaptation to hardship. Out to defend "the black family," these authors argued that babies born out of wedlock created no special problems because these babies were being cared for by a network of female relations.[26] Such views are still heard, albeit less frequently. The basic cause of the problems of the black family, wrote Baptist minister Wallace Smith in 1985, is economic hardship caused by white racism. There is a need to strengthen two-parent families, he conceded, but we must also "develop personhood and positive self-image for those trapped outside the Western accepted model of the family."[27] Stressing the need for new research from an Afrocentric perspective, two professors at Pennsylvania State University have argued that the specific character of black families represents "normative responses to an oppressive social and economic system."[28] Some white social scientists have supported these views and have challenged the superiority of the traditional family.[29] As a concession

25. Quoted (without source) by Paul Taylor in "Life without Father," *Washington Post*, 7 June 1992.

26. See, for example, J. Deotis Roberts, *Roots of a Black Future: Family and Church* (Philadelphia: Westminster Press, 1980), p. 26; cf. Nathan Glazer, *The Limits of Social Policy* (Cambridge, Mass.: Harvard University Press, 1988), p. 25.

27. Smith, *The Church in the Life of the Black Family* (Valley Forge, Pa.: Judson Press, 1985), pp. 41-42.

28. Harold E. Cheatham and James B. Stewart, eds., *Black Families: Interdisciplinary Perspectives* (New Brunswick, N.J.: Transaction, 1990), p. 321.

29. See, for example, William V. D'Antonio, "Family Life, Religion, and Societal Values and Structures," in *Families and Religion: Conflict and Change in Modern Society*, ed. William V. D'Antonio and Joan Aldous (Beverly Hills, Calif.: Sage, 1983), p. 103.

to African-Americans, feminists, gay militants, and others who have argued for the need to tolerate different lifestyles, the 1980 White House Conference on the Family was renamed "Conference on Families." No single set of social arrangements was to have preferred status; society's commitment to the overriding value of the traditional family was abandoned.

In a speech before the U.S. Senate delivered in March 1992, Senator Bill Bradley of New Jersey criticized the silence and distortion that had shaped the issue of race and urban America during the past twenty-five years. All parties, Bradley maintained, had "suffocated discussion of a self-destructive behavior among the minority population in a cloak of silence and denial."[30] A growing number of social scientists and health practitioners agree with this appraisal, and decry the evasion and denial that often characterize discussion of the underclass.

Instead of holding individuals responsible for their conduct, there is a tendency to ascribe the existence of whatever goes wrong to something called "society." In the face of strong evidence to the contrary, much of the conventional wisdom persists in attributing the inner-city epidemic of female-headed families, drugs, violence, and crime to poverty and racism. As a recent study of black Philadelphia has shown, during the decades after the Civil War, despite poverty and racism far worse than that suffered by blacks in Philadelphia today, the black population suffered from relatively few of the structural and social handicaps that now define the underclass. There was a strong network of mutual-benefit and self-help organizations. The great majority of blacks not only believed in but practiced matrimony.[31]

Appeals to a distinctive black culture similarly cannot explain changes over time in the African-American community. In the early 1950s, 74 percent of black mothers had their first child within marriage. The large majority of black mothers with children born out of wedlock eventually married. Even as late as 1970, 30 percent of births to black teens were to married girls.[32] Today, about 25 years later, 90 percent of such births are out of wedlock. In 1907, the percentage of out-of-wedlock births among blacks in Washington, D.C.,

30. Quoted by Daniel Patrick Moynihan in "How the Great Society 'Destroyed the American Family,'" *Public Interest*, no. 108 (Summer 1992): 62.

31. Roger Lane, "Black Philadelphia, Then and Now," *Public Interest*, no. 108 (Summer 1992): 37, 42.

32. Jessica Gress-Wright, "The Contraception Paradox," *Public Interest*, no 113 (Spring 1993): 21.

was 21 percent; in 1991 it stood at 77 percent. In Baltimore it has reached 80 percent.[33] Rates of out-of-wedlock births among blacks have historically been higher than those among whites, but the sharp increases seen during the last twenty years in particular cannot be explained in terms of a specific black culture.

The Problem of the Underclass

Most members of the underclass are living in poverty, but the underclass is not synonymous with the poor. All our cities and many rural areas contain poor people who do not exhibit the characteristics typical of the underclass — family breakdown, teen pregnancy, drug abuse, illiteracy, violent crime, a failure to work, and welfare dependency. These characteristics are most pronounced in the lives of single young people in their late teens and early twenties who are dropouts from both school and the labor force. The underclass, concentrated in urban centers, lives in geographic and social isolation. It is preponderantly black and Hispanic. Its total size is variously estimated at between 2 and 8 million (0.9 to 3.5 percent of the population),[34] but consequences of underclass behavior such as drug abuse, failure in school, and crime affect all of society.

If the underclass is not identical with the poor, neither is it the result of poverty or abandonment by the state. Between 1940 and 1960, as a result of economic growth, the proportion of the American population living in poverty declined by more than half. These were decades during which the welfare state expanded hardly at all. It was during the next twenty years, between 1960 and 1980, when social programs mushroomed, that the underclass emerged in force. This association does not establish a cause-and-effect relationship, but it shows that just as the modern welfare state had succeeded in alleviating most causes of poverty there arose in our inner cities a new form of long-term poverty accompanied by various kinds of self-destructive behavior. Before 1960, rates of poverty were far higher, but crime, single-parent families, and welfare dependency were all much less common than they are today.

33. Moynihan, "The Underclass," p. 22; Nicholas Eberstadt, "Why Babies Die in D.C.," *Public Interest*, no. 115 (Spring 1994): 12-13.

34. Lawrence M. Mead, *The New Politics of Poverty: The Nonworking Poor in America* (New York: Basic Books, 1991), p. 29.

The sociologist William Julius Wilson and others have attributed the growth of the underclass primarily to certain structural trends, notably the disappearance of manufacturing jobs from the central cities and the consequent loss of employment opportunities for unskilled workers. Critics of this thesis have pointed out that the decline in factory jobs cannot explain why members of the underclass fail to take the jobs still available or why they are illiterate and unskilled in the first place. During the height of the 1988-89 boom, when unemployment fell to 5 percent, millions of employable adults did not work. Despite a decline in the proportion of students failing to complete high school and a growth in jobs faster than the growth of the population, there has been a dramatic increase in the percentage of urban males not in the labor force.

According to the careful analysis of Lawrence Mead, none of the structural barriers commonly cited as explanations for the low level of work in the underclass — difficulty in reaching jobs in the suburbs, difficulty in arranging for child care, and so forth — are truly insurmountable obstacles to participation in the labor force. Immigrants from all over the world, many of them uneducated and unskilled, continue to be attracted to this country in search of the opportunities that do exist. The large number of economically successful Asians and West Indian blacks shows that physically distinguishing characteristics do not necessarily stand in the way of acceptance and upward mobility.[35] For example, as a result of hard work, networks of mutual assistance, and a tradition of pride and self-reliance, thousands of Koreans have become successful entrepreneurs, running flower shops, grocery stores, and other businesses. During the last twenty years, hundreds of thousands of black men and women have risen into the middle class, a demonstration of what motivation and the determined pursuit of goals can accomplish. Each success story of a ghetto youth who, in the face of heavy odds, makes something of himself or herself is testimony to the crucial importance of human will. This country continues to have a high rate of social mobility; low-paid workers are not locked into dead-end jobs.

Mead concludes that the chances to get ahead are there, although many in the underclass have indeed become convinced otherwise. "A 'closed opportunity structure' does not exist for most people

35. Cf. Edward Banfield, *The Unheavenly City Revisited* (Boston: Little, Brown, 1974), p. 79.

in America — but it does for those who believe it does."[36] It represents a correct metaphor for the despair that many of the inner-city poor feel about their environment, a despair made worse by the widespread tendency of our society to see poverty as evidence of victimization. By suggesting to the poor of our inner cities that they are the unfortunate playthings of vast economic and historical forces which inevitably grind them to the bottom, we have made them passive and hopeless. "Out of charitable eagerness to absolve them of blame for their condition," writes Myron Magnet in a book tracing the impact of the sixties upon current social policy, "we rob them of the sense of personal responsibility, control and freedom without which no one can summon the energy and initiative to change his fate."[37]

Discussions explaining the emergence of an underclass are often ideologically charged, but both liberals and conservatives agree that there is a culture of poverty. It is characterized by exploitative sexual relationships, early out-of-wedlock childbearing, involvement in drugs and crime, and an inability to hold jobs or an unwillingness to look for work. Liberals argue that these destructive patterns of behavior are for the most part a response to difficult social and economic realities, inadequate schools, and discrimination; they warn against blaming the victim. Conservatives maintain that people should be held accountable for their behavior, regardless of the material and social circumstances in which they live.

A more careful look at the origins and current reality of the underclass may help us find answers to the questions raised by this disagreement. As Lawrence Mead and other analysts of the problem see it, a crucial factor in the rise of the underclass was that, starting in the 1960s, "government largely gave up enforcing orthodox behavior among the urban poor. The schools allowed educational standards to decline, the criminal justice system ceased to deter crime and drug addiction, and — most relevant for this discussion — the welfare system no longer required employable recipients to work."[38] Charles Murray describes the far-reaching effects of these changes:

> In 1960 it was extremely punishing, financially and socially, to have a baby without a husband. The reforms made that behavior less punish-

36. Mead, *The New Politics of Poverty*, p. 158.

37. Magnet, *The Dream and the Nightmare: The Sixties' Legacy to the Underclass* (New York: William Morrow, 1993), p. 116.

38. Mead, *The New Politics of Poverty*, p. 155.

ing on both counts. In 1960, the odds of being caught and going to jail if you committed several crimes were high. The reforms lowered the odds both of being caught and of going to jail. In 1960, public education meant being obliged to comply with a variety of expectations, ranging from actually attending every class, every day, to actually passing examinations. The reforms gutted those requirements.[39]

These social reforms, Murray argues, tore apart the web of rewards and punishments that govern behavior in any community. America had experienced social problems in its urban centers before. Tocqueville described the "rabble" that inhabited the country's major cities. Before World War I, the Irish immigrant population had high rates of fatherless families. However, these kinds of social dislocation then drew the strong disapproval of society. By contrast, following the 1960s, defiance of the ethos of responsibility and impulse-control came to be celebrated, and this cultural revolution proved especially harmful to the poor. The barrage of messages exempting the individual from duty and self-discipline profoundly damaged the chances of the poor to escape from poverty.[40] Teenage pregnancy and dropping out of school became commonplace and more socially acceptable. Until not so long ago, the aim of marriage, including its legal dimension, was to ensure the permanence of unions between adults. Marriage was society's statement that the stability and permanence of such unions are important social values. But the increase and acceptance of unmarried cohabitation became an implicit acknowledgment that society no longer regarded the permanence of the sexual union as truly valuable.[41] These trends now began to feed upon themselves, as Charles Murray pointed out in "The Legacy of the Sixties":

> That a high school does not contain just one girl who is pregnant but many erodes the stigma associated with being single and pregnant, and can even turn into the fashionable thing to do. Holding a low-paying job is something that is admired in a community that depends on precisely such behavior to survive; as the community stops having to depend on that behavior, the praise turns to scorn

39. Murray, "The Legacy of the Sixties," *Commentary*, July 1992, pp. 23-24.
40. Cf. Michael Novak et al., *A Community of Self-Reliance: The New Consensus on Family and Welfare* (Washington, D.C.: American Enterprise Institute, 1987), p. 14.
41. Popenoe, *Disturbing the Nest*, pp. 190-91.

for working for chump change. Trying hard in school becomes a derisively white thing to do when everyone is supposed to be a victim and oppression is a convenient excuse for failure.[42]

Some of the reforms of the 1960s responsible for these changes in social norms have since been modified, but meanwhile the social dynamics of the inner city have taken on a life of their own. The kinds of behavior that have taken root, and which we summarily describe as the culture of poverty, have drawn further strength from society's failure to pass judgment upon these practices when they occur among minority populations. Many of the people of the inner cities, it is agreed, violate the social norms and rules that most Americans regard as reasonable, but they should not really be blamed for this deviant conduct. Among many social scientists in particular there prevails a determinist style of analysis which suggests that members of the underclass cannot be held responsible for their personal behavior. According to this approach (which Mead calls "sociologism"), people are seen as passive. They do not "do" things but rather have things "done" to them. Dropping out of school, becoming addicted to drugs, committing crimes, and having children out of wedlock are behaviors for which the people of the ghettos are "at risk." They "experience" these behaviors rather than initiate them.[43] In this way even rioting can be transformed from an offense into a defense. When the two men who almost killed the truck driver Reginald Denny during the Los Angeles civil disturbances in April 1992 were tried in October 1993, they received only minor punishments. Defense lawyers had argued — successfully, as it turned out — that their clients had been caught up in the spirit of mob violence and therefore could not be guilty of attempted murder.

Several African-American scholars have taken vigorous exception to this approach, which they regard as profoundly disrespectful of the values and capacities of the vast majority of poor black people. The problem of crime is a good case in point. We know from statistics that blacks are far more likely than whites to commit murder, aggravated assault, and robbery.[44] However, it is a fact, as Glenn Loury points out,

---

42. Murray, "The Legacy of the Sixties," p. 24. The "feedback" argument is also stressed by Isabel V. Sawhill, "The Underclass: An Overview," *Public Interest*, no. 96 (Summer 1989), p. 11.

43. Mead, *The New Politics of Poverty*, pp. 129-30.

44. See the figures cited by William Julius Wilson in *The Truly Disadvantaged: The Inner City, the Underclass and Public Policy* (Chicago: University of Chicago Press, 1987), p. 22, and by Jencks in "Is the American Underclass Growing?" p. 78.

that even in the harshest slums the vast majority of blacks are not addicted to crime. Roughly half of all violent crimes are committed by the most active 5 percent of offenders, who are chronic street criminals. Criminal behavior, therefore, can hardly be considered the inevitable result of unemployment, racism, poverty, and/or life in the inner cities. Those who do commit these crimes deserve to be held responsible for their actions.[45] According to Stephen Carter, a professor of law at Yale University, most people of color, "no matter how horrible their life circumstances, refuse to turn to lives of predation. We should not be proud of our society for creating a world in which they are tempted, but we should not confuse the temptations of an unequal society with the coercions of a racially determined one."[46]

The same holds true for the problem of having children out of wedlock. Temptation and impulse are a problem for everyone, but a civilized adult is responsible for what he or she does, regardless of the temptation faced. Certainly not all teenage girls in the ghettos bear children out of wedlock. As we will see in a later chapter, young women who are more religious are less likely to have children outside of marriage. Also, as several studies have shown, parents, teachers, ministers, and upwardly mobile peers can enhance the self-esteem of young women and enable them to resist pressure from boyfriends to engage in sex. "Where personal motivations exist for *not* getting involved with early unwed childbearing," write the authors of a recent Rand study, "young women manage not to."[47] The values and attitudes of young women and their boyfriends have been shown to constitute a critical part of the teen pregnancy story.[48]

The failure of social programs that tried to address the alleged root causes of deviant conduct further weakens the notion that aberrant underclass behavior is the result of a flawed social system rather than the consequence of individual decisions. Between 1965 and 1980, expenditures on social-welfare measures increased from 5 percent to 10 percent of the GNP, and even the conservative climate during the Reagan and Bush era did not result in deep cuts in the size and scope

45. Loury, "The Family as Context for Delinquency Prevention," p. 21.

46. Carter, *Reflections of an Affirmative Action Baby* (New York: Basic Books, 1991), p. 244.

47. Allan F. Abrahamse et al., *Beyond Stereotypes: Who Becomes a Single Teenage Mother?* (Santa Monica, Calif.: Rand, 1988), p. 64.

48. Cf. Loury, "The Family as Context for Delinquency Prevention," p. 16; and Anderson, "Neighborhood Effects on Teenage Pregnancy," p. 386.

CONSEQUENCE OF INDIVIDUAL DECISIONS
RESULT OF FLAWED SOCIAL SYSTEM

of these programs. Overall social spending went right on growing, albeit more slowly than before. For the Head Start program, for example, the increases averaged 15 percent a year under Carter, 5 percent under Reagan, and 22 percent under Bush.[49] Yet despite these massive outlays of money and a multiplicity of social programs designed to do away with the underclass, no headway has been made. Social dislocations such as sexual promiscuity and single-parent families appear to be beyond the reach of remedial government action.

Indeed, numerous studies have shown that even the effects of highly praised programs such as Head Start disappear after about three years. A few experimental programs run by dedicated people have been able to slightly reduce delinquency and pregnancies in later life, but these programs bear little resemblance to Head Start or similar large-scale efforts to reach millions of people.[50] In an essay on the British underclass, Charles Murray made a comment that is equally applicable to the American underclass: "No matter how much money we spend on our cleverest social interventions, we don't know how to make teenagers who have grown up in an underclass culture into steady workers, we don't know how to make up for the lack of good parents, and, most critically, we don't know how to make up for the lack of communities that reward responsibility and stigmatize irresponsibility."[51] Today, as in the eighteenth century, the insight of Dr. Samuel Johnson remains valid:

> How small of all that human hearts endure,
> That part which laws or kings can cure.

Not only have government-run social programs been largely ineffective in the struggle against the culture of poverty, but they have often further weakened traditional structures of support such as ethnic and neighborhood groups, churches, even the family itself. The distribution of condoms in public schools and the availability of abortions without parental consent are cases in point.

There is a growing consensus that the severe social ills associated with underclass life at bottom involve patterns of personal

---

49. Robert Pear, "Social Programs Grow, But Largely by Neglect," *New York Times*, 2 August 1992.

50. Murray, "The Legacy of the Sixties," p. 29.

51. Murray, "The British Underclass," *Public Interest*, no. 99 (Spring 1990): 28.

behavior and defects of character. About 97 percent of those who complete high school, get married and stay married, and work full-time year-round manage to avoid poverty; practically all poverty is associated with the absence of these basic accomplishments. Although poverty plays a role, many problems of the underclass pertain more to internal morale and personal control than to income.[52] Any attempt successfully to address problems such as urban violence, teenage pregnancy, family disruption, and other tragedies will therefore have to concentrate on changing the values and attitudes of individuals. "In the long run," says James Q. Wilson, "the public interest depends on private virtue."[53]

Black people in particular, Glenn Loury has stressed, must learn to accept responsibility for themselves and must restore the values of family, solidarity, and self-help that have enabled them to face and overcome hardships in the past.[54] There is room, and indeed need, for public policies that will strengthen the family, improve education, and protect people against crime. Through no fault of their own, children and young people growing up in the ghettos of our inner cities are at a severe disadvantage, and there are things that government can do to even the odds. But these programs, as social scientist Jewelle Taylor Gibbs has correctly pointed out, will become effective only "if they are supplemented and reinforced by micro-level modifications in family and individual attitudes, values, and behavior within the black community."[55]

Conclusion

The legacy of modernity is one of great accomplishments. Today we live longer, better, and richer lives in every way. In the developed world, modern science and technology have done away with much of the toil

52. This conclusion is one of the central themes of Michael Novak et al. in *A Community of Self-Reliance: The New Consensus on Family and Welfare* (Washington, D.C.: American Enterprise Institute, 1987). See also Novak's essay entitled "Culture First: The New Capitalist Revolution Transformed," in *Being Christian Today: An American Conversation,* ed. Richard J. Neuhaus and George Weigel (Washington, D.C.: Ethics and Public Policy Center, 1992), p. 282.

53. Wilson, "The Rediscovery of Character," p. 16.

54. Loury, "The Moral Quandary of the Black Community," *Public Interest,* no. 79 (Spring 1985): 11-13.

55. Gibbs, "Developing Intervention Models for Black Families: Linking Theory and Research," in *Black Families,* ed. Cheatham and Stewart, p. 347.

and drudgery that not so long ago were the lot of the large majority of people. Modern medicine has eliminated a great deal of disease and suffering. Modern modes of transportation make it possible to rush relief to people struck by disasters such as earthquakes and famine. Modern means of communication enable us to stay in close touch with family members and friends even when they live far away. Inventions such as radio and television bring cultural treasures into our homes and provide entertainment and relief to the sick and aged. In much of the world today, deliberate cruelty to humans and animals is abhorred as never before. People no longer amuse themselves by attending public executions, which in eras past included the drawing and quartering and burning of fellow humans. Last but not least, modernity has given us democracy and the rule of law. In steadily expanding areas of the globe, arbitrary dominion is a thing of the past; governments are held accountable through periodic and free elections. In these societies, religious toleration prevails, and people enjoy the blessings of individual liberty on a previously unimaginable scale. "We live in a world," Charles Taylor has observed, "where people have a right to decide in conscience what convictions to espouse, to determine the shape of their lives in a whole host of ways that their ancestors couldn't control."[56]

But, of course, that is only part of the story. The legacy of modernity also includes much that is harmful to both body and spirit. Modern technology enables us to kill large numbers of human beings with greatly increased efficiency. During the twentieth century, we have experienced previously unheard-of orgies of cruelty and annihilation. As I have tried to show in this chapter, the cultural ethos of radical individualism has become the bane of modern societies. It has undermined traditional values such as civic virtue, family solidarity, and concern for others. The spread of secularism has weakened religious belief and has thereby further eroded traditional kinds of behavior and values such as self-restraint and the control of impulses. It would be simplistic to ascribe the emergence of an inner-city underclass exclusively to changes in values and attitudes, but there can be little doubt that new and corrosive cultural trends have been a crucial factor.

In their pioneering study *Beyond the Melting Pot*, published in 1963, Nathan Glazer and Daniel Patrick Moynihan warned that "no

---

56. Taylor, *The Ethics of Authenticity* (Cambridge, Mass.: Harvard University Press, 1992), p. 2.

effort to change the pattern of Negro low-class family will be effective at a time when the white family is in disorder, when strong families of whatever kind . . . show signs of disintegration."[57] Thirty years later, the link between the crisis of the family and the growth of the underclass has become obvious. As one careful student of the problem has put it, "The most powerful force contributing to the formation of the underclass, perversely enough, may be the changing values of mainstream American society, in which the virtues of family stability, mutual support, and religiously based commitment to the marriage vow no longer command the deference they once did."[58] Unless this trend is reversed, the number of children born to unmarried white women will continue to climb, and there is the distinct possibility that we will witness the emergence of a large white underclass. Illegitimacy, Charles Murray has warned, "is the single most important social problem of our time — more important than crime, drugs, poverty, illiteracy, welfare or homelessness because it drives everything else." American society, Murray argues, "could survive when illegitimacy became epidemic within a comparatively small ethnic minority. It cannot survive the same epidemic among whites."[59]

Can we expect a reversal of the crisis of values that is sweeping modern society? Is it possible to overcome the predominance of expressive individualism, the preoccupation with what has been called the "untrammeled self"? I will address these questions in the final chapter of this book.

57. Glazer and Moynihan, *Beyond the Melting Pot: The Negroes, Puerto Ricans, Jews, Italians, and Irish of New York City*, 2nd ed. (Cambridge, Mass.: MIT Press, 1970), p. 84.

58. Paul E. Peterson, "The Urban Underclass and the Poverty Paradox," in *The Urban Underclass*, ed. Jencks and Peterson, p. 19.

59. Murray, "The Coming White Underclass," *Wall Street Journal*, 29 October 1993.

RED   YELLOW

SUPERSTITION   MYSTICAL/SUPERSTITION
─────────────   ──────────────────────
REASON   REASON
RATIONAL

4. Is America Becoming a More Secular Society?

Ever since the Enlightenment of the eighteenth century, numerous Western intellectuals have predicted the demise and eventual disappearance of religion. Advances in scientific knowledge, they have argued, would drive out belief in supernatural powers and would inevitably lead to a secular age, the triumph of reason over superstition. At the end of the nineteenth century, Friedrich Nietzsche concluded that the greatest event of his time was the realization that "God is dead" — that belief in the Christian God is no longer tenable. More recently, many philosophers and the great majority of social scientists have embraced the ideology of secularism, the promotion of the decline of religion. According to two students of the subject, illustrious figures in sociology, anthropology, and psychology have "expressed confidence that their children, or surely their grandchildren, would live to see the dawn of a new era in which, to paraphrase Freud, the infantile illusions of religion would be outgrown."[1]

And yet, as we will soon see in more detail, social reality in the United States in particular has failed to conform to these predictions. Religion is alive and well and shows no signs of disappearing from the scene. It is estimated that on any given Sunday there are more people in churches than the total number of people who attend professional sporting events in an entire year. There are about 500,000 local churches and synagogues voluntarily supported by the American people.[2] According to a Gallup poll taken in 1993, 59 percent of

1. Rodney Stark and William Sims Bainbridge, *The Future of Religion: Secularization, Revival, and Cult Formation* (Berkeley and Los Angeles: University of California Press, 1985), p. 1.
2. Peter L. Berger and Richard John Neuhaus, *To Empower People: The*

Americans consider religion "very important" in their lives. An additional 29 percent said that religion was "fairly important," and only 12 percent indicated that it was "not very important."[3]

Of course, compared with, say, the fifteenth or the sixteenth century, the twentieth century is a more secular age. In the past, the power of religious ideas was due in large measure to their ability to explain things. God was invoked to solve the mystery of the origin of the universe; the order of nature itself called forth a sense of gratitude to the deity and an acknowledgment of divine providence. Today the regularities of nature as well as numerous other phenomena are accounted for in the language of the natural sciences. The steady accumulation of empirical knowledge has provided new modes of explanation for everything from the weather to disease to human behavior. Theology, once the queen of the sciences, remains the concern of the clergy and others professionally concerned with religious questions, but its dominant hold over human affairs has ended. God has become a distant and impersonal entity that seemingly plays a greatly reduced role in the world. In the societies of the West, religious faith, once part of the ethos of society, has become a private affair. There has been a growing elimination of religious values and symbols from the conduct of public discourse; Richard John Neuhaus has spoken of a "naked public square."[4]

The term "secularization" provides a summary description of the changes in worldview that have emerged during the last few centuries. According to the American sociologist Peter Berger, who is indebted to the work of Max Weber, the causes of secularization must be sought not only in the new and influential role of scientific thought but also in different concrete social experiences that characterize contemporary life — industrialism, capitalism, and bureaucracy. "These social formations of modernity," he asserts, "bring about habits and mind-sets which are unfavorable to the religious attitude. They en-

Role of Mediating Structures in Public Policy (Washington, D.C.: American Enterprise Institute, 1977), p. 27.

3. George Gallup, Jr., and Robert Bezilla, "More Find Religion Important," Washington Post, 22 January 1994.

4. Cf. Neuhaus, The Naked Public Square: Religion and Democracy in America (Grand Rapids, Mich.: William B. Eerdmans, 1984). See also Bryan Wilson's "Secularization: The Inherited Model," in The Sacred in a Secular Age: Toward Revision in the Scientific Study of Religion, ed. Phillip E. Hammond (Berkeley and Los Angeles: University of California Press, 1985), pp. 12-13.

courage activism, problem-solving, this-worldliness, and by the same token they discourage contemplation, surrender, and a concern for what may lie beyond this world." Whereas at one time people lived in cohesive communities that provided a stable base for accepted ways of thinking, large numbers of people now are concentrated in impersonal cities. Large-scale mobility contributes to a rootless existence that further undermines moral and religious homogeneity and certainty.[5]

The new secular worldview is particularly strong among Western intellectuals, a new elite of society since the days of the Enlightenment. Because intellectuals play a powerful role in the dissemination of knowledge through education and the mass media, the entire tone of society has become more overtly secular. And yet it would be a mistake to deduce from this development that religious faith is generally weakening and that religion is about to disappear. There is no evidence of a simple linear decline in the social prominence or cultural influence of religion. Whether measured by church membership, attendance at church services, professed belief in God, or any number of other social indicators, aggregate trends do not show a continuing and irreversible process of secularization.[6]

Church Membership and Attendance

As Table 4.1 shows, the number of Americans who are members of churches or synagogues has held steady over the last fifty years; fluctuations have been minor. Attendance at religious services, too, has been relatively stable for the past generation. In a poll taken in 1959, 49 percent of Americans indicated that they had attended a church or synagogue during the previous seven days. In 1991, this figure stood at 42 percent.[7] According to a recent study, many more Americans

---

5. Berger, "For a World with Windows: Hartford in Sociocultural Context," in *Against the World and for the World: The Hartford Appeal and the Future of American Religion,* ed. Peter L. Berger and Richard John Neuhaus (New York: Seabury Press, 1976), pp. 10-11.

6. This is the conclusion of many observers of the religious scene, including Robert Wuthnow. See his book entitled *The Restructuring of American Religion: Society and Faith since World War II* (Princeton, N.J.: Princeton University Press, 1988), p. 297.

7. Princeton Religion Research Center, *Religion in America: 1992-1993* (Princeton, N.J.: Princeton Religion Research Center, 1993), pp. 42-43.

TABLE 4.1
Percentage of Adults Who Say They Are Members
of a Church or Synagogue

Year	Pct.	Year	Pct.
1938	73	1978	68
1939	72	1979	68
1940	72	1980	69
1942	75	1981	68
1944	75	1982	67
1947	76	1983	69
1952	73	1984	68
1965	73	1985	71
1975	71	1986	69
1976	71	1987	69
1977	70	1991	68

Source: Gallup poll[8]

claim to attend church services than actually do,[9] but this disparity probably does not affect the observed stability of attendance. Most of the change that has occurred stems from a sharp decline in attendance among Catholics. Between 1958 and 1985, church attendance for Catholics dropped from 74 to 53 percent. Some observers attribute this slump to Pope Paul's encyclical *Humanae Vitae* on birth control, but during the last decade, attendance has been stable and may actually be rising. Patterns of church attendance among Protestants have shown little change.[10]

The 1960s did show a decrease in religious participation and interest. Both church membership and church attendance peaked and then began to decline. In part, this was a result of the general cultural climate of that decade, a time of disillusionment and rebellion. As a consequence of an unpopular war, large numbers of Americans expe-

8. Ibid., p. 39.

9. C. Kirk Hadaway et al., "What the Polls Don't Show: A Close Look at U.S. Church Attendance," *American Sociological Review* 58 (1993): 741-52.

10. Cf. Andrew M. Greeley, *Religious Change in America* (Cambridge, Mass.: Harvard University Press, 1989), pp. 45-48. See also the book by George Gallup, Jr., and Jim Castelli entitled *The American Catholic People: Their Beliefs, Practices, and Values* (Garden City, N.Y.: Doubleday, 1987), p. 42.

rienced deep alienation from the values and traditions of their country. Attachment to organized religion, especially the mainline churches, was one of the casualties. The new commitment to personal freedom and choice eroded loyalty to the religious establishment. Increased rates of divorce and more permissive attitudes toward sex were some of the symptoms of the cultural revolution. Disenchantment with the American way of life was accompanied by a flourishing consumer culture that weakened older religious norms. Self-gratification and enjoyment of life became ends in themselves. These new cultural trends began among the young, but by the late 1970s they had spread into much of middle-class America.[11]

By 1980, the situation had stabilized, and organized religion showed signs of recovery. Conservative religious denominations had begun to show important gains in membership. It turned out that the weakening of religious affiliation experienced in the previous two decades had not been part of a general process of secularization. In large measure, argues sociologist Andrew Greeley, it may have been a phenomenon caused by younger Americans. Younger people, as we will see in more detail later, are generally less attached to religion.[12]

Other indicators reinforce the conclusion that while a portion of the population has become less religious, another part has become more religious. Indeed, as Table 4.2 shows, the size of the highly religious group is greater than that of the group claiming to have "no religion." The compiler of this table, analyzing these and other data, concludes that "secularization seems to have ceased in the 1980s and may be reversing. The cessation or reversal may be temporary, but it is inconsistent with the view that continuous secularization is inevitable in modern societies."[13]

A comprehensive national survey of the American population, conducted between April 1989 and April 1990, showed that 86.5 percent are Christians. Among the rest, 7.5 percent said they had no religion, .7 percent considered themselves agnostics, and .02 percent were humanists.[14] A 1988 Gallup poll gave the number of Americans without

11. Cf. Wade Clark Roof and William McKinney, *American Mainline Religion: Its Changing Shape and Future* (New Brunswick, N.J.: Rutgers University Press, 1987), pp. 13-46, 61-62.

12. Greeley, *Religious Change in America*, pp. 31-33.

13. Ibid., p. 311.

14. Barry A. Kosmin, *The National Survey of Religious Identification 1989-90* (New York: City University of New York Graduate Center, 1991).

TABLE 4.2

Comparison of Lower-Tail and Upper-Tail Indicators of the Religiousness of the U.S. Adult Population, 1972-84

Date	% of Respondents Who Said They Had No Religion	% of Respondents Who Said They Attended Religious Services Several Times a Week
1972	5.2	6.3
1973	6.4	7.5
1974	6.8	7.9
1975	7.6	6.9
1976	7.6	8.9
1977	6.1	8.1
1978	7.8	8.1
1980	7.2	7.5
1982	7.3	8.4
1983	7.3	8.5
1984	7.3	9.3

Source: The General Social Surveys conducted by the National Opinion Research Center[15]

a self-declared religious preference as 10 percent.[16] This number may be somewhat larger than poll data indicate. In this country, a stigma is attached to being unchurched, and in some instances individuals may tell pollsters what they think a good American should tell them. On the other hand, the fact that a person is not a member of a church or does not regularly attend religious services does not necessarily indicate lack of religious belief. As several studies show, a majority of individuals who say they have no religious affiliation believe in the supernatural and mystical. Only a relatively small percentage of them are secular rationalists.[17]

15. The table is taken from Norval D. Glenn's article entitled "The Trend in 'No Religion' Respondents to U.S. National Surveys, Late 1950s to Early 1980s," *Public Opinion Quarterly* 51 (1987): 309.

16. George H. Gallup, Jr., and Jim Castelli, *The People's Religion: American Faith in the 90s* (New York: Macmillan, 1989), pp. 68-69.

17. Stark and Bainbridge, *The Future of Religion*, p. 47. See also Glenn M. Vernon's essay entitled "The Religious 'Nones': A Neglected Category," in *Journal for the Scientific Study of Religion* 7 (1968): 219-29.

A 1980 study of the unchurched defined them as all those not on the rolls of Christian religious bodies and divided them into several groups. Some are members of non-Christian religions, sects, or cults such as Judaism, Buddhism, and Islam. Some have been active members of Christian churches but, for various reasons, no longer belong or practice their religion. Many members of this subgroup consider church members to be hypocrites and not truly religious. Some of the unchurched have never belonged to a religious organization. Lastly, there are the atheists, agnostics, and humanists, who constitute the smallest segment of the unchurched. The author of this investigation concluded that being unchurched in America does not necessarily imply being irreligious.[18]

In 1846 Abraham Lincoln is supposed to have stated, "I am not a member of any Christian church, but I have never denied the truth of the Scriptures."[19] Many contemporary Americans could make the same statement. A study published in 1978, which defined the unchurched as all those who attended church once a year or less, found that a majority of them believed in life after death. Among Protestant unchurched, 60 percent held this belief; among Catholic unchurched, 53 percent. Even among those with no religious preference, 41 percent believed in life after death.[20] Gallup poll figures for 1988 indicated that 25 percent of the unchurched (compared with 40 percent of the churched) had various kinds of religious experience — a feeling of union with a divine being, visions, a sudden turning to God, and the like. Belief in Jesus Christ as the son of God was affirmed by 72 percent of the unchurched (compared with 84 percent of the churched).[21] A study of Presbyterians who had been confirmed in Presbyterian churches in the 1950s and 1960s showed that in 1989-90, 48 percent were no longer affiliated with the Presbyterian Church or any other denomination. But when asked whether Jesus was God or the son of God, whether the Bible was divinely inspired, and whether there was life after death, 72 percent of these people said yes to all three ques-

18. J. Russell Hale, *The Unchurched: Who They Are and Why They Stay Away* (New York: Harper & Row, 1980), pp. 51, 97-98.
19. Quoted by Nathan O. Hatch in "Sola Scriptura and Novus Ordo Seclorum," in *The Bible in America: Essays in Cultural History,* ed. Nathan O. Hatch and Mark A. Noll (New York: Oxford University Press, 1982), p. 59.
20. David A. Roozen, *The Churched and Unchurched in America: A Comparative Profile* (Washington, D.C.: Glenmary Research Center, 1978), p. 26.
21. Gallup and Castelli, *The People's Religion,* pp. 68, 140.

TABLE 4.3
Membership Changes in Evangelical and Mainline Churches, 1973-1994

MAINLINE CHURCHES

	1973	1994	Change
United Methodist Church	10,192,265	8,584,125	-16%
Episcopal Church	2,917,165	2,504,682*	-14%
Christian Church			
(Disciples of Christ)	1,330,747	937,644	-29%
United Church of Christ	1,867,810	1,501,310	-20%

EVANGELICAL CHURCHES

	1973	1994	Change
Southern Baptist Convention	12,295,400	15,614,060	+27%
Church of Jesus Christ of			
Latter-Day Saints (Mormons)	2,569,000	4,613,000	+79%
Assemblies of God	1,099,906	2,324,615	+111%
Seventh-Day Adventists	476,276	775,349	+63%
Church of the Nazarene	417,732	597,841	+43%

Source: *Yearbook of American and Canadian Churches*[22]
*Data for the Episcopal Church is for the year 1993.

tions.[23] Clearly, it would be a mistake to consider the unchurched simply as unbelievers.

An indication of the religious revival under way since the 1970s is the decrease in membership in the mainline Protestant churches and the rapid growth of conservative denominations (see Table 4.3). The gradual decline of religious groups that modernize their doctrines and embrace temporal values is of course not new. Ever since the early days of the Republic, such churches have lost their vigor, and their members have defected to less worldly sects. For many decades, the large mainline Protestant denominations have represented a steadily decreasing fraction

22. *Yearbook of American and Canadian Churches: 1975* (Nashville: Abingdon Press, 1975), Table 1-A; and *Yearbook of American and Canadian Churches: 1996* (Nashville: Abingdon Press, 1996), Table 2.

23. "Protestant Baby Boomers Not Returning to Church," *New York Times*, 7 June 1992.

of total church membership; from the 1970s on, they began to experience a decline in absolute numbers as well. On the other hand, religious groups that stress the comforting of souls and motivate sacrifice have, historically, done well.[24] Particularly striking in recent years has been the increase in the number of evangelicals who describe themselves as "born-again Christians," commit themselves to spread the gospel, and believe in the literal interpretation of the Bible. Enrollments in evangelical schools and colleges have climbed; evangelical radio and television stations have multiplied. At the end of the 1970s, estimates put the number of evangelicals at one-fifth of the American electorate.[25] While at one time evangelicals had been passive and withdrawn from politics, the new-style evangelism was assertive and became an increasingly influential force in the life of the nation. In 1976, a born-again Southern Baptist, Jimmy Carter, won the presidency.

The trend is unmistakable: the mainline Protestant churches continue to lose members while churches committed to a return to traditional values and a stress on salvation through personal commitment to Christ gain adherents. In a world burdened by moral uncertainties, membership in a conservative church offers moral confidence and sureness. A growing number of Americans, it appears, reject the compromises made by the mainline churches with contemporary fads such as complete sexual freedom, the acceptance of homosexuality as just another lifestyle, and abortion on demand. These individuals also seek a sense of community and fellowship and oppose the inroads of secular worldviews and the weakening of transcendent elements in the Christian tradition. As one observer puts it, "If all the churches offer is psychotherapy and politics, no wonder that those who seek God will turn elsewhere."[26]

It is likely that the sharp drop in church attendance among Roman Catholics and the decline in the number of young Catholics entering seminaries and joining religious orders during the last two decades is related to the same antisecular impulse. Since Vatican Council II in the 1960s, the Catholic Church has discarded cherished distinctions in the

24. This is the central argument of Roger Finke and Rodney Stark in their important book entitled *The Churching of America, 1776-1990: Winners and Losers in Our Religious Economy* (New Brunswick, N.J.: Rutgers University Press, 1992).

25. Cf. Robert C. Liebman, "The Making of the New Christian Right," in *The New Christian Right: Mobilization and Legitimation,* ed. Robert C. Liebman and Robert Wuthnow (New York: Aldine, 1983), p. 234.

26. Berger, "For a World with Windows," p. 18.

TABLE 4.4
Percentage of Americans Who Say Religion Is
"Very Important" in Their Lives

Year	Total	Protestants	Catholics
1952	75%	76%	83%
1965	70	74	76
1978	52	60	51
1987	53	60	54
1991	58	NA	NA
1993	59	NA	NA

Source: Gallup poll[27]

areas of liturgy, theology, and lifestyle, and has become more "mainline." The result has been an erosion of the power of traditional symbols and sacraments, a loss of priestly authority, and a consequent drop in religious commitment on the part of Catholic parishioners.[28]

Values and Beliefs

As pollsters acknowledge, public-opinion surveys are not able to do full justice to the spiritual element and depth inherent in moral values and doctrinal beliefs, but they do provide a good indication of overall trends. The picture that emerges from these polls is sometimes complex, but it contradicts any notion of general secularization. Large numbers of Americans continue to believe in a personal God, Judgment Day, life after death, and so on.

According to 1993 Gallup poll data, 88 percent of Americans that year regarded religion as "very important" or "fairly important" in their lives. As Table 4.4 indicates, the number of those who see it as "very important" has declined over the last thirty-five years, though since the early 1980s the trend has again reversed itself. A Gallup poll of 1993 showed that 59 percent of Americans considered religion "very important."[29]

27. Gallup and Bezilla, "More Find Religion Important," *Washington Post*, 22 January 1994; cf. Gallup and Castelli, *The People's Religion*, pp. 39, 61.
28. Cf. Finke and Stark, *The Churching of America*, pp. 247-72.
29. Gallup and Bezilla, "More Find Religion Important."

There are other indications of a relative decline in the importance of religion. In 1957, 81 percent of Americans thought that religion could provide solutions to all or most of life's problems. By 1991, this percentage had declined to 59 percent. In 1963, 65 percent said that they regarded the Bible as "the actual word of God and [that it] is to be taken literally, word for word." In 1991, only 32 percent took this position.[30] Most of this decline is accounted for by a drop in the acceptance of the literal truth of the Bible on the part of Catholics, whose religious teaching does not hold them to strict literalism.[31]

And yet a persistence of and even an increase in religious beliefs and practice can be observed in regard to many other measures of religious commitment. Bible reading and biblical knowledge have increased modestly. In 1986, one-third of all adult Americans read the Bible at least once a week, and one in nine read it daily. Since the end of World War II, the percentage of Americans who say that they believe in God or a universal spirit has never dropped below 90 percent; in 1986 it stood at 94 percent. In 1978, 78 percent regarded Jesus as God or the son of God; in 1988, 84 percent saw Jesus in this way. Since 1944, the belief that there is life after death has been held by about 70 percent of adult Americans. In the mid-1980s, about 75 percent of Americans surveyed prayed at least once a week. Close to 90 percent believed that God loved them. More than 75 percent said that religious involvement had been a positive experience in their lives. None of these acknowledgments of the importance of religion depended upon church membership or attendance of church services.[32]

Every year between 1979 and 1988 (except for 1986), Americans expressed more confidence in their church than in any other major social institution. In 1988, organized religion was ranked as deserving the highest confidence by 59 percent of the American population. Fifty-eight percent gave this rating to the military, 56 percent to the Supreme Court, 49 percent to the public schools, 36 percent to newspapers, 27 percent to television, and 26 percent to organized labor.[33] Since 1988, when the scandals involving Jim Bakker, Jimmy Swaggart, and other television

30. Princeton Religion Research Center, *Religion in America: 1992-1993*, p. 22.

31. Greeley, *Religious Change in America*, p. 19.

32. Gallup and Castelli, *The People's Religion*, pp. 45, 63; George Gallup, Jr., and Sarah Jones, *100 Questions and Answers: Religion in America* (Princeton, N.J.: Princeton Religion Research Center, 1989), pp. 15-16, 40-41, 206-7.

33. Gallup and Castelli, *The People's Religion*, p. 43.

TABLE 4.5
Support for Traditional Social Values

	Welcome	Not Welcome	No Opinion
More family ties			
1978	91%	5%	4%
1981	92	5	3
1988	94	3	3
More respect for authority			
1978	89	6	5
1981	89	6	5
1988	89	7	4
More sexual freedom			
1978	29	62	9
1981	25	67	8
1988	22	68	10
More marijuana acceptance			
1978	20	74	6
1981	13	82	5
1988	8	87	5

Source: Gallup poll[34]

evangelists began to unfold, confidence in the honesty and ethical standards of the clergy has slipped slightly. However, it is still higher than that accorded to doctors and college teachers, and it is well above the rating given to lawyers and members of Congress.[35]

Between 1978 and 1988, respect for traditional social values gained broader public support. Gallup poll surveys conducted in 1978, 1981, and 1988 (see Table 4.5) brought forth the above answers to the question "Here are some social changes which might occur in coming years. Would you welcome these or not welcome them?"

Table 4.5 reveals that most Americans favor stronger family ties and greater respect for authority while a declining percentage support more sexual freedom and greater acceptance of marijuana. Changes

34. Adapted from Gallup and Jones, *100 Questions and Answers*, p. 102.
35. Cf. "Tarnished Halos," *New York Times*, 21 November 1992. This article reports on a survey undertaken in June 1992 by the Princeton Religion Research Center.

between 1978 and 1988 show increasing support for the kinds of values endorsed by the more conservative Christian churches.

The Role of Age and Education

Religious interest and activity increase with age. Young people, predominantly single, are relatively less interested in religion because they are occupied with establishing their own lives and often experiment with breaking away from the religion in which they were raised. Marriage, on the other hand, usually leads to greater involvement with a church; 90 percent of Americans with children between the ages of four and eighteen want religious instruction for their children.[36]

As people get older and become more aware of their own mortality, religious commitment increases. Gallup poll data for 1991 show that whereas 46 percent of Americans under 30 years of age considered religion "very important" in their lives, 70 percent of those 50 years and older valued religion in this way.[37] Part of the increased interest in religion that we noted earlier may therefore be the result of a larger older population; as longevity increases, so will the number of more religious people. There is also the phenomenon of the baby boomers — the 76 million Americans born between 1946 and 1964, constituting the largest generation in American history — who are maturing; many of them are now returning to churches and synagogues.[38]

Over the last fifty years, the number of Americans who graduate from high school and go on to college has increased sharply, and this fact, too, has ramifications for the role of religion in American society. On the whole, it appears, religious commitment decreases as the educational level increases. For example, as Table 4.6 shows, those with more education consider religion to have less importance in their lives, while those with less education place more importance on religion.

36. Ibid., pp. 50-51.

37. Princeton Religion Research Center, *Religion in America: 1992-1993*, p. 55.

38. Cf. Peter Steinfels, "Beliefs," *New York Times*, 6 January 1990. See also Wade Clark Roof's *A Generation of Seekers: The Spiritual Journeys of the Baby Boom Generation* (San Francisco: HarperSanFrancisco, 1993).

TABLE 4.6
Importance of Religion among Differently Educated Groups

	College Graduate	High-School Graduate	Less Than H.S. Graduate
Very important	50%	58%	68%
Fairly important	29	31	23
Not very important	20	10	8

Source: Gallup poll[39]

There are other areas in which increased education correlates with decreased religious activity or belief:

- 40 percent of those who did not graduate from high school read the Bible at least once a week; only 28 percent of those with education beyond high school do so.
- 45 percent of those who did not graduate from high school see the Bible as the literal word of God; only 11 percent of college graduates hold this view.
- 90 percent of those with a high-school degree or less believe that Jesus is God or the son of God; only 66 percent of college graduates hold this belief.
- 40 percent of those who did not graduate from high school describe themselves as born-again Christians; only 22 percent of college graduates so describe themselves.[40]

The fact that individuals with more education score lower on certain measures of religious commitment does not prove, of course, that exposure to education actually causes less involvement with religion. The basic values of young people are generally quite resilient and little affected by instruction in the schools. Decisive changes in their outlook on the world — feared by conservatives and hoped for by radicals — are seldom achieved. This conclusion appears strengthened by the finding that with regard to some other measurements, either education makes no difference or college graduates actually show greater interest in religion:

39. Princeton Religion Research Center, *Religion in America: 1992-1993*, p. 55.
40. Gallup and Castelli, *The People's Religion*, pp. 86-87. These figures are based on poll data from the late 1980s.

- 91 percent of college graduates believe in God, almost the same percentage as that of those who did not graduate from high school (93 percent).
- 69 percent of college graduates believe in life after death; 67 percent of those who did not graduate from high school hold this belief.
- 74 percent of college graduates are church members; 69 percent of those with high-school degrees or less are members.
- 46 percent of college graduates attend church in a given week; only 37 percent of those who did not graduate from high school attend weekly.[41]

Studies of the religious orientation of scientists illustrate the complexity of the issue we are looking at here. Several of these investigations indicate that scientists have less religious involvement, are less likely to believe in God, and so on. Similarly, among college faculties there seems to exist a negative relationship between various measures of religious commitment and scholarly orientation and the quality of the institution at which these faculty members are teaching.[42] However, other findings cast doubt upon the idea of a necessary conflict between science and religion.

As I noted in the first chapter, in the seventeenth and eighteenth centuries, religion actually encouraged the rise of modern science. Today, despite great advances in astronomy and astrophysics, many students of cosmology show interest in religious explanations of the origin of the universe. As it turns out, the more exact scientific disciplines, such as physics and chemistry, have higher rates of religiosity among their practitioners than do the less scientific specialties such as the social sciences and the humanities. A 1974 study of faculty members showed that whereas 49 percent in the social sciences and 46 percent in the humanities were indifferent or opposed to religion, only 37 percent in the physical sciences took this view. One interpreter of these data suggests that people in the social sciences and humanities reject religion not so much because of what they dislike about religion specifically, but because of the need they feel to maintain the plausibility of their scientific orientation. Because they are in "soft" disciplines, these individuals seek

41. Ibid., pp. 59, 87-88.
42. Cf. Robert Wuthnow, "Science and the Sacred," in *The Sacred in a Secular Age*, ed. Hammond, pp. 188-89.

to differentiate themselves from the uneducated and religious general public by adopting a hostile attitude toward religion.[43]

Other studies of scientists and students reveal that it is the irreligious who select academic careers in the first place. Academic life does not cause these individuals to become less religious; rather, they are less religious before they ever enter academic life. Again, this situation is especially pronounced among students and practitioners of the social sciences and humanities. Finally, and of particular importance for the question of cause-and-effect relationships and future trends, studies done over several decades do not show that the extremely rapid growth of science in recent times has been accompanied by a correspondingly sharp decrease in religiosity.[44] The period of time since World War II has shown rapid increases in expenditures on research and development and on higher education as well as in the number of college and advanced degrees awarded. Yet when we look at the total picture of religiousness in America, declines in religious participation and religious belief, where they have occurred at all, have been modest, and countervailing trends are present as well.

Conclusion

In certain ways, America today is a more secular society than it was several generations ago, yet the prediction of a linear progression toward increasing secularization is unsupported by the evidence available. Contrary to the predictions of rationalists and positivists, religion has not been rendered superfluous by modern science. Not being primarily a matter of cognitive belief or assertion, religious faith has been left largely untouched by the growing range and importance of scientific knowledge. Religious belief, it appears, is deeply imbedded in people's existential situation; it is part of the human condition — a response to the uncertainties of human life. It was described this way by sociologists Rodney Stark and William Bainbridge, two thoughtful students of the future of religion:

> Only the gods can assure us that suffering in this life will be compensated in the next. Indeed, only the gods can offer a next life

43. Ibid., pp. 196-98.
44. Ibid., p. 191.

— an escape from individual extinction. Only the gods can formulate a coherent plan for life, that is, make meaningful in a fully human way the existence of the natural world of our senses. . . . We see no reason to suppose that the diffusion of science will make humans in the future less motivated to escape death, less affected by tragedy, less inclined to ask, "What does it all mean?" True, science can challenge *some* of the claims made by historic religions, but it cannot provide the primary satisfactions that have long been the raison d'être of religions.[45]

Believing Christians will add other, more theological explanations for the persistence of their religion in modern society. Some of them will be dissatisfied with a theoretical construct that anchors the phenomenon of religion in certain universal human needs and thus, at least by implication, assigns equal importance to all religions. Yet the truth or falsity of a particular religious creed is not the issue before us. Our perspective here, unlike that of atheism, is essentially agnostic. While it views religion *sub specie temporis*, it leaves unanswered the questions of whether and how religion might also be viewed *sub specie aeternitatis*. As Peter Berger observes, "To say that religion is a human projection does not logically preclude the possibility that the projected meanings may have an ultimate status independent of man."[46]

Atheists, too, take issue with a theory of religion that sees religion as part of the human condition. The fact that many people need the consolations of religion, writes the secular humanist Kai Nielsen, "reveals something about how *they* were brought up and nothing about the very condition of man."[47] Sidney Hook, another philosopher committed to atheism, argued that religion persists because of the failure of human beings to be rational: "The revival of religion today is not due to the discovery of new arguments or evidence for supernaturalism or a profounder analysis of the logic of religious belief. . . . The religious renaissance of our time is really

45. Stark and Bainbridge, *The Future of Religion*, p. 431. See also Robert N. Bellah's essay entitled "The Historical Background of Unbelief," in *The Culture of Unbelief: Studies and Proceedings from the First International Symposium on Belief Held at Rome, March 22-27, 1969*, ed. Rocco Caporale and Antonio Grumelli (Berkeley and Los Angeles: University of California Press, 1971), pp. 39-52.

46. Berger, *The Sacred Canopy: Elements of a Sociological Theory of Religion* (Garden City, N.Y.: Doubleday, 1967), p. 181.

47. Nielsen, *An Introduction to the Philosophy of Religion* (London: Macmillan, 1982), p. 62.

part of the more inclusive movement of irrationalism in modern thought."[48]

The argument that all truly rational individuals will regard belief in the supernatural as a superstition, on the same level as the magic of primitive people, involves a considerable degree of intellectual arrogance. An agnostic, adopting a sociological perspective, will take the less presumptuous view that while some individuals undoubtedly can live without feeling a need for religion, the ultimate disappearance of religion is highly unlikely. In the future, religious expression will undoubtedly take many new and different forms, but because religious faith plays such a crucial role in providing a sense of purpose and meaning in life, such changes are unlikely to lead to universal secularization.

The flourishing of evangelical Protestantism and the growth of cults such as the Unification Church are direct results of the failure of the more traditional churches to address the questions that men and women have always asked about the meaning of human existence. Stark and Bainbridge observe that "while the mainline denominations discard the traditional confessions, clash over the ordination of women and homosexuals, and often seem to regard the government of South Africa as the central religious matter of the day (and in so doing, alienate thousands more of their current members), other movements, both sects and cults, are dealing in a far richer expression of the supernatural."[49] These religious organizations prosper because the conventional churches have become too worldly and no longer meet the spiritual aspirations of large numbers of Americans. They respond to unfulfilled religious needs and provide a sense of identity and community. In response to the moral uncertainties of a society caught in skepticism and relativism, they offer a stricter morality and a new moral absolutism. Whether these new groups at some point will supplant the mainline organizations, nobody can tell today.

While recent American history confutes the prophecy of inevitable secularization, and while much of the Third World experiences an upsurge of religiousness, Western Europe appears to be dominated by a secular impulse. According to Gallup poll data for 1981, reproduced in Table 4.7, religious commitment is far weaker on the Continent than it is in the United States.

48. Sidney Hook in the symposium "Religion and the Intellectuals," *Partisan Review* 17 (1950): 96-97.
49. Stark and Bainbridge, *The Future of Religion*, p. 447.

TABLE 4.7
Religious Belief in Western Europe and the U.S.

	Importance of God in Life (Scale 1-10)	Belief in Life after Death
Sweden	3.99	N.A.
Denmark	4.47	26%
France	4.72	35
West Germany	5.67	39
Great Britain	5.72	45
Italy	6.96	47
United States	8.21	71

Source: Gallup poll[50]

Various explanations have been advanced for what appears to contradict the theory of the pervasiveness of religion. Established European churches, argues Andrew Greeley, have often been identified with feudalism, class privilege, and monarchical absolutism. In response to the churches' defense of reaction, Europeans developed a strong strain of anticlericalism, frequently perceiving organized religion as an enemy. The United States, on the other hand, has no history of feudalism or monarchy; here, established churches soon gave way to the separation of church and state and religious pluralism. In this setting, religion carries none of the pejorative baggage of European churches and indeed has functioned as an important source of personal identity. Hence, concludes Greeley, it is the apparent failure of Christianity in Europe that constitutes the deviant case. Europe, not the United States, is unique. It is Europe that for various historical reasons exhibits trends contrary to the usual role of religion in society.[51]

Other students of the subject point out that European countries, while they have lower rates of religious involvement and belief than the United States, do have majorities that believe in God. According to the Gallup poll of 1981, 87 percent of people in Spain, 76 percent in Great Britain, 72 percent in West Germany and Norway, 65 percent in the Netherlands, and 58 percent in Denmark do believe

50. George H. Gallup, "Religion in America: 50 Years, 1935-1985," *Gallup Report*, no. 236 (May 1985): 50 and 53.
51. Greeley, *Religious Change in America*, pp. 117-18, 121.

in God.[52] Acceptance of the moral precepts of Christianity continues to be widespread among large numbers of Europeans.[53] In recent years, perhaps as a reaction to the prevailing impersonal practice of religion, a growing number of people have flocked to Europe's major religious shrines. Many Catholics, it appears, look for spiritual experience and renewal. Between 1983 and 1992, the number of visitors to Lourdes, for example, increased from 4 million to 5.5 million.[54] While traditional religious denominations often encounter considerable indifference on the Continent, various American-based movements such as the Mormons, Jehovah's Witnesses, and the Assemblies of God report great success there. Denmark and Sweden surpass the United States in their receptivity to Scientology. There are more Indian and Eastern cult centers in Europe than in the United States; the countries with the lowest rates of involvement with these cults are the largely Catholic countries — Belgium, Italy, and Spain — in which the Roman Catholic Church remains influential. In some cases, left-wing politics serve as the functional alternative to sect and cult movements, and in countries with serious left-wing movements, some of the energy that might otherwise be channeled into religion will be diverted to these causes.[55]

Whatever the reasons for the lower religiousness of Western Europe, as foreign observers since Alexis de Tocqueville have noted, the United States has long been one of the most religious countries in the Christian world, and this situation has not changed appreciably over the years. As Tocqueville saw it, ever since colonial times Americans have combined the spirit of religion and the spirit of liberty. Religious beliefs have remained interwoven in the American creed of individual rights, equality, and freedom. Their persistence, argues Everett Carll Ladd, a student of public opinion, demonstrates that industrial civilization does not necessarily disrupt religion: "Aspects of the social and political experience obviously led to a decline of religious belief and practice in a number of industrial countries, but it was not

52. These and other relevant data can be found in the appendix of *Unsecular America*, ed. Richard John Neuhaus (Grand Rapids, Mich.: Wm. B. Eerdmans, 1986).

53. Cf. Stephen Harding et al., *Contrasting Values in Western Europe: Unity, Diversity, and Change* (London: Macmillan, 1986), p. 70.

54. Marlise Simons, "Pilgrims Crowding Europe's Catholic Shrines," *New York Times*, 12 October 1993.

55. Stark and Bainbridge, *The Future of Religion*, pp. 476-84, 503.

the process of development per se that brought about this decline. The United States has not repealed or confounded the laws of history; it has simply arrived at modernity through a route different from that followed by most other countries."[56] In other words, modernity is not inevitably synonymous with secularization. While individuals committed to secularist ideas occupy many influential positions in American culture, the United States as a whole remains a highly religious society.

SPIRT OF RELIGION — COMMUNITY
SPIRIT OF LIBERTY — INDIVIDUAL

---

56. Ladd, "Secular and Religious America," in *Unsecular America*, ed. Neuhaus, p. 20.

RELIGIOUS PIETY
MORAL GOODNESS

5. Religiousness and Moral Conduct: Are Believing Christians Different?

At least 86 percent of the American people consider themselves Christians, and some of them speak of this country being a Christian nation. But does adherence to the Christian religion affect their behavior? Does the Christian faith transform at least the lives of those who take their religion seriously and whom we may want to call believing Christians?

Few Christian thinkers today claim a necessary link between religious piety and moral goodness. There is no inevitable connection between religious belief and morally good behavior, write two Catholic observers of American life: "Being good and being religious are separate and distinct."[1] It is a truism of daily experience, argues the Catholic theologian Eric D'Arcy, that many individuals can act morally without religious belief and that believers can commit immoral acts: "Many an atheist is honest and chaste and reliable, unselfish, generous, and kind. On the other hand, many a believer has been dishonest and unjust, insensitive to the feelings of his own family or to the needs of the poor."[2] "That persons can have praiseworthy moral characters without being religious or, particularly, Christian," notes the Protestant theologian James Gustafson, "cannot be gainsaid."[3] The socialization process that shapes moral thinking involves many factors, not all of

1. Germain Grisez and Russell Shaw, *Beyond the New Morality: The Responsibilities of Freedom* (Notre Dame: University of Notre Dame Press, 1974), p. 190.

2. D'Arcy, " 'Worthy of Worship': A Catholic Contribution," in *Religion and Morality: A Collection of Essays*, ed. Gene Outka and John P. Reeder, Jr. (Garden City, N.Y.: Doubleday, 1973), p. 194.

3. Gustafson, *Can Ethics Be Christian?* (Chicago: University of Chicago Press, 1975), p. 80.

87

them of a religious nature. Some theologians invoke the theological concept of "general revelation" — the idea of a God-created moral order that is accessible to all people — in order to explain this phenomenon.

Many of these same thinkers not only disavow the notion that one has to be a Christian in order to be good, but also question whether religious belief has much of an effect on moral conduct. "While religion is highly popular in America," observe two students of American public opinion, "it is to a large extent superficial; it does not change people's lives to the degree one would expect from their level of professed faith."[4] The deeds of Christian saints and martyrs are, of course, evidence that the Christian faith has the power to transform individual lives. Living a life of faith, writes Gustafson, can alter the values a person holds. Indeed, there are grounds "for questioning the integrity and wholeness of one's own life if one purports to be Christian but does not bear some marks in one's moral character of that living and believing."[5] At the same time, Christian writers hesitate to claim that Christians are in any sense better human beings than their non-Christian neighbors. At most one finds an occasional assertion that nonreligious persons considered morally praiseworthy are so considered because their conduct coincides with an implicit Judeo-Christian norm.

Not surprisingly, atheists and secular humanists vigorously deny that personal virtue or social conduct generally are in any way dependent upon religious faith. "There is no evidence," wrote Algernon Black, the longtime senior leader of the New York Society for Ethical Culture, "that those who believe in the traditional God concepts are more law-abiding or respecting of their fellows or considerate of society than those who have turned from theism."[6] According to Sidney Hook, there are no grounds for assuming that belief in the existence of the supernatural is an essential condition for public order or private morality. "Among those who are moved by fear," he claimed, "fear of the Lord is not as potent as fear of the Law in inhibiting immoral impulses."[7]

Hook argued that the link between religion and morality could

4. George H. Gallup, Jr., and Jim Castelli, *The People's Religion: American Faith in the 90s* (New York: Macmillan, 1989), p. 21.

5. Gustafson, *Can Ethics Be Christian?* p. 80.

6. Black, "Our Quest for Faith: Is Humanism Enough?" quoted in Paul W. Kurtz, ed., *The Humanist Alternative: Some Definitions of Humanism* (Buffalo, N.Y.: Prometheus Books, 1973), p. 73.

7. Hook, *Education for Modern Man: A New Perspective*, rev. ed. (New York: Alfred A. Knopf, 1963), p. 157.

be subject to empirical tests, but he made no effort to seek out social-science literature dealing with this issue. The secular humanist philosopher Paul Kurtz claimed to have consulted such literature, and he presented to his readers the finding that those who pray do not commit fewer crimes. In 1984, in what must surely be considered one of the most egregious misunderstandings of statistical data, Kurtz wrote, "Research studies have shown that the lowest percentage of inmates in prisons are freethinkers and unbelievers or individuals from such backgrounds, and that the highest percentage are from religious backgrounds."[8] Since 89.4 percent of Americans are Christians, Jews, Muslims, or belong to other religions that practice prayer, and since freethinkers constitute no more than a tiny segment of the American population (less than 1 percent)[9], Kurtz's finding was, of course, hardly surprising. At the same time, it tells us nothing whatsoever about any cause-and-effect relationship between religion and morality.

There are many anecdotal accounts of how religious belief affects moral conduct. The newspapers often print stories about Christian ministers and priests as well as other dedicated Christian men and women who sacrifice time and comfort in order to see to the needs of the poor and homeless. In Memphis, Tennessee, Kenneth Bennett, a white evangelical Christian, has organized a service he calls "Streets," which provides black teenagers in the city's run-down public housing projects with a variety of constructive programs. "My faith calls me to do this," Bennett explains, and he adds, paraphrasing James 2:17, "Faith without works is death."[10] Among the good Samaritans who rescued truck driver Reginald Denny after he had been dragged from his truck and severely beaten during the Los Angeles riots in April 1992 was Bobby C. Green. After seeing the attack on Denny on his television, Green explained, he acted because "I think God told me to get up and go there."[11] Yet those who want to find confirmation for the moral evil they regard as linked to or caused by religion will also not be disappointed. In 1989, a former

8. Kurtz, "Is Prayer Essential to Morality?" *Free Inquiry*, Summer 1984, pp. 5-6.

9. Cf. *The National Survey of Religious Identification 1989-90*, a study directed by Barry A. Kosmin (New York: Graduate School and University Center of the City University of New York, 1991). This survey, one of the largest ever undertaken, has been widely praised. See the article by Ari L. Goldman entitled "Portrait of Religion in U.S. Holds Dozens of Surprises," *New York Times*, 10 April 1991.

10. Peter T. Kilborn, "Where the Young Are Stranded in Poverty, a Good Samaritan Stops His Van," *New York Times*, 31 January 1993.

11. "Doctor Testifies on Beating in Riot," *New York Times*, 5 August 1992.

Seventh-Day Adventist minister and his wife went on trial in Pennsylvania, charged with the death of their fourteen-year-old son, who had gone without food for six weeks. After the minister had lost his job as a truck driver, the couple had refused to spend any of their $3,775 in savings on groceries because they considered the money a tithe for God.[12] In the late 1980s, proponents of secularism had a field day after Jim Bakker, the head of the PTL ministry, which had an annual budget of $129 million, was sentenced to forty-five years in prison for fraud, and after another well-known television evangelist, Jimmy Swaggart, was defrocked amidst charges of sexual involvement with a prostitute.

And yet there is no need to rely on this kind of anecdotal evidence. Ever since the fathers of modern social science, Emile Durkheim and Max Weber, first analyzed the role of religion in shaping society and human behavior, sociologists, psychologists, criminologists, and other social scientists have been gathering data and writing about the relationship of religion and human conduct; there is now a large and still-growing body of empirical literature. A review of all articles published in ten major sociological journals between 1960 and 1969 alone found 185 articles examining the role of religious beliefs and values in influencing behavior.[13]

To be sure, much of the early literature was methodologically deficient and therefore of little worth. Investigators failed to define or use consistently key terms such as "religion," "religious," and "religiousness." Many of the groups studied were too small to allow generalization. The selection of samples was often inadequate. Many of the studies did not have comparison groups; few of them used statistical techniques such as analysis of variance and regression in order to rule out spurious relationships. In 1963, in a pioneering study of the impact of religion on social life, Gerhard Lenski noted, "Less systematic sociological research has been devoted to religion than to any other major institution of our society."[14] In 1971, in a review of the literature dealing with juvenile delinquency, crime, and religion, the authors concluded, "Most research done in this area is insignificant scientifically."[15]

12. "Girl Testifies for Parents," New York Times, 9 September 1989.

13. Gary D. Bouma, "Assessing the Impact of Religion: A Critical Review," Sociological Analysis 31 (1970): 172-79.

14. Lenski, The Religious Factor: A Sociological Study of Religion's Impact on Politics, Economics, and Family Life, rev. ed. (Garden City, N.Y.: Doubleday, 1963), p. 2.

15. Richard D. Knudten and Mary S. Knudten, "Juvenile Delinquency, Crime and Religion," Review of Religious Research 12 (1971): 147.

During the last two decades, the technical sophistication of social-science research, including that dealing with the religious factor, has improved considerably. Some of this research still takes up very narrowly circumscribed topics of little general importance. A highly technical apparatus and the impressive precision of the results often hide the triviality of the subject matter. Outside critics, bewildered by the jargon-laden language of much of this literature, level the charge of mindless number-crunching. There also arise difficult questions of cause and effect, to which we will return. Nevertheless, it would be wrong to ignore this body of knowledge entirely. Using nontechnical language, I will review the most important findings of this research under several headings.

Juvenile Delinquency

An important event in the recent history of social-science research on the role of religion was the publication in 1969 of the article "Hellfire and Delinquency" by the highly respected researchers Travis Hirschi and Rodney Stark. This work, characterized by a sophisticated research design, appeared to be beyond challenge on methodological grounds.

Hirschi and Stark sought to answer the question of whether religion in contemporary society has much to do with developing or sustaining personal ethics. Indeed, they asked, "Is the Christian sanctioning system of hellfire for sinners and heavenly glory for the just, able to deter unlawful behavior even among those who are firm believers?" Using a sample of 4,077 junior and senior high-school students from Western Contra Costa County, California, Hirschi and Stark found that belief in the existence of a supernatural world and church attendance were essentially unrelated to delinquency. "Students who attend church every week are as likely to have committed delinquency acts as students who attend church only rarely or not at all." The roots of morality for law-abiding students, they concluded, were attachment to and love of one's neighbor as well as awareness of and concern for the real-life costs of crime. "The church is irrelevant to delinquency," they asserted, "because it fails to instill in its members love of their neighbors and because belief in the possibility of pleasure and pain in another world cannot now, and perhaps never could, compete with the pleasures and pains of everyday life."[16]

16. Hirschi and Stark, "Hellfire and Delinquency," *Social Problems* 17 (1969): 202-13. The quoted passages are on p. 211 and pp. 212-13.

The conclusions that Hirschi and Stark reached in "Hellfire and Delinquency" contradicted much previous research on the subject. At least since Durkheim's study of suicide in 1897, which had stressed the importance of the "moral community," social scientists had come to see religion as an important force in instilling moral convictions and ensuring and maintaining social norms. Indeed, as recently as 1967, the sociologist Joseph Fitzpatrick had identified religion as one of the primary factors in socialization. Consequently, he argued, a strong religious family life is "the most effective protection against delinquency."[17] The new findings also ran counter to commonsense views of juvenile wrongdoing. One tends to assume that a young person who believes in an afterlife and the prospect of eternal bliss or damnation would take into account the rewards associated with lawful behavior and the punishments associated with delinquency. Nevertheless, the conclusion of Hirschi and Stark that church attendance and belief in supernatural sanctions were not significant predictors of delinquency soon became part of the conventional wisdom and found its way into undergraduate textbooks.

Yet this was not to be the last word on the subject. Several subsequent studies that sought to replicate the work of Hirschi and Stark yielded different results. Using the same measures of religiousness on a sample of high-school students in the Pacific Northwest in 1974, Steven Burkett and Mervin White found a strong inverse relationship between church attendance, moral values, and respect for worldly authority and the use of alcohol and marijuana. Religiousness, they concluded, had no clear effect on the offenses chosen by Hirschi and Stark — larceny, vandalism, and assault — that are condemned by most segments of secular society as well. But it did have consequences for adolescents' use of drugs and alcohol — practices that are condoned by many secular individuals and are not heavily penalized in many jurisdictions, but to which the churches had maintained their opposition in a more forthright manner.[18]

Findings different from those of Hirschi and Stark were also reported by Paul Higgins and Gary Albrecht in 1977. Their study of high-school students in Atlanta, Georgia, showed a moderately negative relationship between church attendance and seventeen measures

17. Fitzpatrick, "The Role of Religion in Programs for the Prevention and Correction of Crime and Delinquency," in *Task Force Report: Juvenile Delinquency and Youth Crime* (Washington, D.C.: Government Printing Office, 1967), p. 322.

18. Burkett and White, "Hellfire and Delinquency: Another Look," *Journal for the Scientific Study of Religion* 13 (1974): 455-62.

of delinquency. They surmised that the different findings were the result of geographical factors — religion had more of an effect in the South, where it occupied a more central place in people's lives and where church attendance therefore indicated a stronger commitment to Christian moral values.[19] In another study published in the same year, Stan Albrecht and his associates found religious participation and religious attitudes among Mormon teenagers in three western states to be moderately strong predictors of avoidance of deviant conduct, especially victimless deviance such as drug and alcohol abuse.[20] Also published in 1977 was a study by two Canadian researchers who partially replicated the Hirschi and Stark study among Calgary youth between the ages of fifteen and twenty-four. They found that those who attended church most frequently had the lowest degree of illicit drug use.[21] A study of high-school students in Arizona published in 1979 showed that, irrespective of denominational differences, church attendance had the greatest inverse relationship to delinquency.[22]

By 1982, Stark himself conceded the significance of the accumulated evidence. Religion, he admitted, had potent effects on delinquent and deviant behavior, though these effects varied with the religious climate of the community studied: "Where the surrounding community is permeated by religious beliefs and concerns, variations in individuals' religiousness will influence delinquency. But where the surrounding community is highly secular, the effects of individuals' religiousness will be muffled and will not influence delinquency."[23] This conclusion was congruent with the findings of other investigators who had noted the importance of peers. Stark put it this way in another article published in 1984:

19. Higgins and Albrecht, "Hellfire and Delinquency Revisited," *Social Forces* 60 (1977): 952-58.

20. Albrecht et al., "Religiosity and Deviance: Application of an Attitude-Behavior Contingent Consistency Model," *Journal for the Scientific Study of Religion* 16 (1977): 263-74.

21. Rick Linden and Raymond Lurrie, "Religiosity and Drug Use: A Test of Social Control Theory," *Canadian Journal of Criminology* 19 (1977): 346-55.

22. Gary F. Jensen and Maynard L. Erickson, "The Religious Factor and Delinquency: Another Look at the Hellfire Hypothesis," in *The Religious Dimension*, ed. Robert Wuthnow (New York: Academic Press, 1979), pp. 157-77.

23. Stark et al., "Religion and Delinquency: The Ecology of a 'Lost' Relationship," *Journal of Research in Crime and Delinquency* 19 (1982): 15.

It is not whether an individual kid goes to church or believes in hell that influences his or her delinquency. What is critical is whether the *majority* of the kid's *friends* are religious. In communities where most young people do not attend church, religion will not inhibit the behavior even of those teenagers who personally are religious. However, in communities where most kids are religious, then those who are will be less delinquent than those who aren't.[24]

The "ecological" factor also explained why the 1969 study by Hirschi and Stark, conducted in secularized California communities, had shown no connection between religiousness and delinquency: it had failed to take into account the religious climate of the communities examined. In addition, as other data revealed, such highly secularized communities are the exception rather than the rule, and, for the nation as a whole, Stark concluded, "religion serves to undergird the moral order. The results are as Durkheim supposed, and are consistent with what many juvenile judges who have ordered delinquents to attend church and Sunday school have taken for granted."[25]

Stark argued that at least one of the reasons why it had taken years to confirm this commonsense view was that the "overwhelming majority of social scientists were irreligious or even anti-religious. This led them to believe that religion was a disappearing and unimportant factor in human affairs." To acknowledge that religiousness helps prevent delinquency implies a positive judgment of religion. "Moreover," Stark noted, "if it were widely known that religiousness does restrain delinquency, some people would be bound to suggest that religious training ought to be encouraged because of these social benefits. Given the private attitudes toward religion predominant among social scientists, most probably would not want to lend encouragement to such proposals."[26] A similar view had been expressed a few years earlier by Donald Campbell, the president of the American Psychological Association. Present-day psychology and psychiatry, he declared in his presidential address in 1975, "are more hostile to the inhibitory messages of traditional religious moralizing than is scientifically

---

24. Stark, "Religion and Conformity: Reaffirming a Sociology of Religion," *Sociological Analysis* 45 (1984): 274-75.

25. Ibid., p. 14.

26. Stark et al., "Religion and Delinquency: The Ecology of a 'Lost' Relationship," p. 22.

justified."[27] Given these attitudes, it is not surprising that data showing religion in a positive light have often been ignored by social-science researchers.

The weakening of the secularist trend during the last decade may be one reason for the greater openness to religious explanations that can be observed in recent social-science research. In 1986, Douglas Sloane and Raymond Potvin concluded that a measure of religiousness that combines church attendance and the perceived role of religion in daily life is "a potent device for distinguishing nonoffenders, occasional offenders, and frequent offenders with respect to each of a dozen different forms of delinquent behavior."[28] "Both research and theory," noted Charles Peek and his associates in an article published in 1985, "are converging on the conclusion that high religiosity deters delinquent conduct."[29] Surveying a large body of research, John Cochran and Ronald Akers concluded in 1989 that the demonstrable effects of religion were consistent enough to provide support for this generalization: "Religiosity is inversely related to delinquent behavior."[30]

Adult Crime

There exists no generally agreed-upon definition of crime. The annual reports on crime in the United States published by the FBI rely on information received from thousands of sheriffs and police chiefs throughout the country. Law-enforcement agencies define and keep records of crime in their jurisdiction in many different ways. Still, the differences in reporting crime generally cancel each other out and do not prevent us from studying the relationship of religiousness and criminality.

In 1985, a review of 56 research studies dealing with the link between religiousness and crime revealed substantial evidence of an

27. Campbell, "On the Conflicts between Biological and Social Evolution and between Psychology and Moral Tradition," *American Psychologist* 30 (1975): 1103.

28. Sloane and Potvin, "Religion and Delinquency: Cutting through the Maze," *Social Forces* 65 (1986): 90.

29. Peek et al., "Religiosity and Delinquency over Time: Deviance Deterrence and Deviance Amplification," *Social Science Quarterly* 66 (1985): 120.

30. Cochran and Akers, "Beyond Hellfire: An Exploration of the Variable Effects on Adolescent Marijuana and Alcohol Use," *Journal of Research in Crime and Delinquency* 26 (1989): 221.

inverse relationship. The author, Lee Ellis, found that these studies utilized various measures of religiousness. Some involved overt behavior such as church membership and church attendance. Others used categories such as belief in God or in an afterlife with divine sanctions. The studies also operated with different categories of criminality, and contradictory findings for the most part were accounted for by these divergent measures of religiousness and criminality. Ellis concluded that in view of the multiplicity of factors involved, there was no simple answer to the question "Do religious people commit fewer crimes?" Nevertheless, one finding stood out: If by being religious "one means attending church frequently, there is manifestly a strong tendency for religious people to commit fewer crimes."[31]

This finding is in line with what one would expect in view of several theoretical assumptions about the social role of religion. To an important degree, the criminal law of a society reflects the moral principles of the religion of the majority of its population. Strong adherence to religion, therefore, should result in fewer violations of the law. Most religions also teach that violations of moral principles will result in sanctions in the afterlife; accordingly, strong adherents of religion can be expected to commit fewer offenses. Religiousness also reflects a general inclination to obey authority.

There are several comprehensive studies of religion and adult crime rates in American society. In a study published in 1980, Rodney Stark investigated the relationship of church membership and crime in standard metropolitan statistical areas (SMSA's) — defined as cities with 50,000 or more inhabitants and urbanized areas that have at least 50,000 inhabitants. Controlling for other variables such as age, unemployment, poverty, and racial composition, Stark found a significant negative correlation (-.44) between rates of church membership and overall crime rates. The correlation was lowest for homicide and assault — crimes of impulse and/or passion that are less governed by bonds to the moral order. Stark theorized that measures of private faith such as prayer and reading of the Bible were less important for shaping the moral climate of metropolitan areas than the proportion of people belonging to churches. "For faith to influence behavior it must do so through creating a moral *climate*, and this requires the social expres-

31. Ellis, "Religiosity and Criminality: Evidence and Explanations of Complex Relationships," *Sociological Perspectives* 28 (1985): 513.

sion of religion. Church membership directly measures the social embodiment of religion."[32] Stark concluded that the data examined "suggest that nineteenth-century social scientists were correct about the central role played by religion in sustaining the moral order. Cities with higher proportions of church members have lower rates of crime than do more secular cities."[33]

Another study, undertaken by William Bainbridge and published in 1989, showed similar results. Using data from 75 American metropolitan areas outside of New England with populations over 500,000, Bainbridge found significant negative associations between church membership and three crimes — assault, burglary, and larceny. Controlling for other variables such as age, education, racial composition, and income, Bainbridge concluded that religion has "an independent power to deter several kinds of deviant behavior in which harm is done to other persons."[34] Most recently, T. David Evans and his associates found that religious activities such as attending church, listening to religious broadcasts, and reading religious materials had a significant negative effect on adult criminality.[35]

Two other researchers, Steven Stack and Mary Kanavy, studied the incidence of rape in the fifty states. Their study, published in 1983, showed that the religious factor was the variable most closely associated with the variance in the frequency of rape. Specifically, they found that the greater the percentage of Catholics in a state, the lower the rate of rape. This finding survived multiple regression analysis — that is, factors drawn from prominent criminological theories such as economic condition, race, and age turned out to be insignificant variables, while Catholicism (followed by alcoholism) remained the most important predictor of rape rates. The authors concluded that "the greater the intensity of the bond between an individual and religion the lower the probability of deviant behavior."[36]

32. Stark et al., "Rediscovering Moral Communities: Church Membership and Crime," in *Understanding Crime: Current Theory and Research*, ed. Travis Hirschi and Michael Gottfredson (Beverly Hills, Calif.: Sage, 1980), p. 45.
33. Ibid., p. 50.
34. Bainbridge, "The Religious Ecology of Deviance," *American Sociological Review* 54 (1989): 292.
35. Evans et al., "Religion and Crime Reexamined: The Impact of Religion, Secular Controls and Social Ecology on Adult Criminality," *Criminology* 33 (1995): 195-224.
36. Stack and Kanavy, "The Effect of Religion on Forcible Rape," *Journal for the Scientific Study of Religion* 22 (1983): 68.

TABLE 5.1
1993 Violent Crimes per 100,000 Population

	United States	Mountain States	Utah
Violent Crime	746	589	301
Murder	9.5	6.4	3.1
Robbery	256	130	59
Aggravated assault	440	410	195

Source: *Statistical Abstract of the United States: 1995*, Table 310, p. 200[37]

This conclusion is confirmed by a study of white-collar workers undertaken in 1992 by Professor Robert P. Wuthnow of Princeton University. Using questionnaires and in-depth interviews, Wuthnow found that those who seldom or never attended church services stole postage stamps and used office equipment for personal purposes and committed other similar unethical, not to say criminal, acts more frequently than those who were regular churchgoers. Significantly, the 20 percent of workers who reported membership in small religious groups meeting for Bible study, prayer, self-help, or community action were least likely to bend the rules. Peter Steinfels, the *New York Times* reporter describing this research, noted, "Not long ago, no one would have thought that a sociological study was required to prove that religiously active employees were apt to be honest. That was before Jim Bakker and Jimmy Swaggart."[38]

Findings demonstrating the relevance of the religious factor receive additional confirmation from figures on crime in Utah. In that state, about 75 percent of the population belong to the Church of Jesus Christ of Latter-Day Saints, and Mormons are known for their strong religious convictions and commitment to traditional social values. Utah's rate of urbanization, an important predictor of crime, is above the national average; the average age of its inhabitants (lower than the national average) should also be conducive to a high crime rate. Yet Utah is one of the safest states in the nation in terms of violent crime in

37. See also Richard E. Johnson's essay entitled "Crime," in *Utah in Demographic Perspective: Regional and National Contrasts*, ed. Thomas K. Martin et al. (n.p.: Signature Books, 1986), p. 279.

38. Steinfels, "Churchgoing Affects Office Ethics (But Few Are Truly Saints)," *New York Times*, 28 February 1993.

particular, as Table 5.1 indicates. We do not know the religious affiliation of those residents of Utah who committed the crimes of violence included in these statistics. Yet in the absence of other explanations, it is not unreasonable to assume that Utah's low rate of violent crime is related to the state's strong religious tradition, its identification with the Mormon church. Everything we know about the relationship of religiousness and crime indicates that the greater the participation in religion, the lower the probability of criminal behavior.

Prejudice and Intolerance

Research on prejudice and religion has shown consistently that church members and church attenders are more prejudiced than those not regularly attending church services. One of the first such studies, undertaken by Harvard social psychologist Gordon Allport and published in 1946, revealed that students who claimed no religious affiliation were less likely to be "anti-Negro" than those who declared themselves to be Protestant or Catholic.[39] Replicating this study in 1949, J. F. Rosenblith discovered the same phenomenon in South Dakota.[40] The authors of *The Authoritarian Personality*, published in 1950, showed that church attenders had significantly higher scores of ethnocentrism and authoritarianism than nonattenders.[41] Similarly, Samuel Stouffer discovered that church attendance was linked to more than ethnic prejudice: he found that church members who had attended services within the past month were more intolerant of nonconformists such as socialists, communists, and atheists than those who had not attended.[42] Numerous other studies as well as public-opinion polls have confirmed the central finding that religious people show more prejudice and intolerance than nonreligious people. According to General Social Surveys data, compiled by the National Opinion Research Center (NORC) at the University of Chicago, con-

39. G. W. Allport and B. M. Kramer, "Some Roots of Prejudice," *Journal of Psychology* 22 (1946): 9-39.

40. Rosenblith, "A Replication of 'Some Roots of Prejudice,'" *Journal of Abnormal and Social Psychology* 44 (1949): 470-89.

41. T. W. Adorno et al., *The Authoritarian Personality* (New York: Harper, 1950).

42. Stouffer, *Communism, Conformity and Civil Liberties: A Cross Section of the Nation Speaks Its Mind* (Garden City, N.Y.: Doubleday, 1955).

servative Protestants are consistently the least supportive of individual liberties and rights for blacks.[43] Relevant research has established that this relationship holds even when factors such as education, age, and region of the country are taken into account.[44]

Several explanations have been advanced for the link between religion and prejudice and intolerance. In *The Authoritarian Personality*, T. W. Adorno and his associates argued that religion and prejudice have common causes. In their view, individuals accept religion because they are given to conformity and submission to authority. Prejudice and intolerance are natural expressions of tendencies toward conventionalism and thinking in in-group/out-group terms, especially where the general culture fosters prejudice. Others have suggested that strong religious involvement by its very nature fosters prejudice. As is most obvious in the case of small sects, claims of exclusive access to divine truth and the strong emotional involvement present in these groups create suspicion and occasionally hostility toward those who do not share the group's beliefs.[45]

In some cases, churches embrace beliefs which imply that some groups are unworthy and inferior. In their book entitled *Christian Beliefs and Anti-Semitism*, Charles Glock and Rodney Stark argued that a significant proportion of modern anti-Semitism was due to church teachings about the Jews. They suggested that historical images of the Jews as apostates and as the crucifiers of Christ continued to produce a hostile view of the contemporary Jew. Negative images of Jews, they found, were especially pronounced among conservative Protestants.[46] Subsequent students of the subject have questioned whether Glock and Stark succeeded in demonstrating a cause-and-effect relationship between Christian orthodoxy and anti-Semitism. In any case,

43. See the data cited in Wade Clark Roof and William McKinney's *American Mainline Religion: Its Changing Shape and Future* (New Brunswick, N.J.: Rutgers University Press, 1987), pp. 191-97, and David A. Roozen's *The Churched and Unchurched in America: A Comparative Profile* (Washington, D.C.: Glenmary Research Center, 1978), pp. 43, 49-51, which is based on NORC data.

44. Cf. the studies cited by Gordon W. Allport and J. Michael Ross in "Personal Religious Orientation and Prejudice," *Journal of Personality and Social Psychology* 5 (1967): 433, and Stouffer, *Communism, Conformity and Civil Liberties*, p. 147.

45. Michael Argyle and Benjamin Beit-Hallahmi, *The Social Psychology of Religion* (London: Routledge & Kegan Paul, 1975), pp. 115-17.

46. Glock and Stark, *Christian Beliefs and Anti-Semitism* (New York: Harper, 1966), pp. 63-66.

as I noted in the first chapter, the Roman Catholic Church and other Christian bodies in recent years have acknowledged the theological roots of anti-Semitism and have taken steps to modify certain traditional religious teachings.

While secularist-minded social scientists occasionally have dwelt with glee on the observed relationship between religion and prejudice, others have taken a more nuanced view. Gordon Allport, the first researcher to discover the link, spoke of a "grand paradox" in an article entitled "Personal Religious Orientation and Prejudice":

> One may not overlook the teachings of equality and brotherhood, of compassion and humanheartedness, that mark all the great world religions. Nor may one overlook the precept and example of great figures whose labors in behalf of tolerance were and are religiously motivated — such as Christ himself . . . and many others, including the recently martyred clergy in our own South. These lives, along with the work of many religious bodies, councils, and service organizations would seem to indicate that religion as such *unmakes* prejudice. A paradox indeed.[47]

In this important article, published in 1967, Allport and his Harvard colleague J. Michael Ross also drew attention to the curvilinear relationship between church attendance and prejudice: frequent church attenders were less prejudiced than infrequent attenders and often less prejudiced than nonattenders. If religion as such caused only prejudice, one would expect to find that those who exposed themselves to its influence most constantly would be the most prejudiced. But such was not the case. Several studies revealed that casual and irregular fringe members of churches were the most prejudiced. A recent study based on Gallup poll data has confirmed this finding. It showed that the 13 percent of the population who on a twelve-item scale scored "highly spiritually committed" were more tolerant than those on the lower part of the scale.[48]

Allport and Ross suggested that the apparent paradox could be resolved by paying attention to the personal motives and attitudes of those attending church. These were not all the same: There were churchgoers *and* there were churchgoers. Using a series of questions

47. Allport and Ross, "Personal Religious Orientation and Prejudice," p. 433.
48. George H. Gallup, Jr., and Timothy Jones, *The Saints among Us* (Harrisburg, Pa.: Morehouse, 1992), p. 41.

about the role of religion in a person's life, Allport and Ross were able to show that the regular and frequent attenders, who went to church once a week or more, were more likely to be people who internalized the values of humility, compassion, and love of neighbor. Irregular and infrequent attenders, on the other hand, found religion to be a useful tool in gaining friends and influence; it was not something integral to their personal lives. Frequently it offered them both a defense against existential anxiety and solace, a way of gaining security and social opportunities. Allport and Ross called these two types of religious outlook and orientation intrinsic and extrinsic. "Perhaps the briefest way to characterize the two poles of subjective religion is to say that the extrinsically motivated person *uses* his religion, whereas the intrinsically motivated *lives* his religion."[49] Small wonder, they concluded, that the intrinsically motivated churchgoers were significantly less prejudiced than the extrinsically motivated. For both types, religion was knit into the fabric of their personalities. But while human kindness was as essential as belief in God for intrinsically religious persons, extrinsically religious persons easily succumbed to inducements to bigotry. Nothing in their religious outlook required a surrender of pet prejudices.

It has been argued that the intrinsic-extrinsic typology of religiousness does not explain why those without any religious affiliation are generally more open-minded and tolerant than churchgoers.[50] In 1971, the Yale psychologist James Dittes suggested that much of the correlation between prejudice and religion may be due to factors of education and class.[51] Two other researchers, who had reviewed several dozen studies and twenty-five years of research into the issue of religion and prejudice, concluded in 1974 that "it is still not possible to specify the direction of influence between personality variables, religious com-

---

49. Allport and Ross, "Personal Religious Orientation and Prejudice," p. 434. The authors described a third type whom they called indiscriminately proreligious. This person, characterized by undifferentiated thinking and dogmatism, was found to be the most prejudiced. The indiscriminately proreligious person was an essentially insecure type, unable to make fine distinctions and given to scapegoating.

50. Argyle and Beit-Hallahmi, *The Social Psychology of Religion,* p. 115.

51. Dittes, "Religion, Prejudice, and Personality," in *Research on Religious Development: A Comprehensive Handbook,* ed. Merton P. Strommen (New York: Hawthorn, 1971), p. 363. See also the book by Dittes entitled *Bias and the Pious: The Relationship between Prejudice and Religion* (Minneapolis: Augsburg, 1973).

mitment, and prejudice."[52] Sixteen years later, in 1990, two other social scientists concurred with this appraisal and recommended the development of more sophisticated approaches and new scales of measurement.[53] Yet despite these reservations about the work of Allport and Ross, the central conclusion and policy implication of their groundbreaking research can probably stand: One important way in which a nominally Christian society can make headway against prejudice and intolerance is to take seriously the teachings of equality and fraternity that are highly valued by its religious faith.

Single Parenthood among Teenagers: Children Having Children

Some feminists take the position that women should not have to marry men in order to have babies, but there has developed a near consensus among health professionals that single (unwed) parenthood is bad for children. Controlling for low income and other associated problems, researchers have found strong evidence that such children are more likely to experience a variety of behavioral and educational difficulties.[54] Damaging consequences are especially pronounced in the case of unwed teenage mothers. There are, first, negative consequences for the young mothers themselves, which will leave an imprint on their offspring. These young women will earn less as adults because most of them will drop out of school after becoming pregnant. They will have psychological difficulties because their normal maturational process will be interfered with. And many of these teen mothers will have more children out of wedlock and will spend substantial parts of their adult lives on welfare. According to a Congressional Budget Office report, 77 percent of unmarried adolescent mothers were welfare re-

52. Richard L. Gorsuch and Daniel Aleshire, "Christian Faith and Ethnic Prejudice: A Review and Interpretation of Research," *Journal for the Scientific Study of Religion* 13 (1974): 289.

53. Lee A. Kirkpatrick and Ralph W. Hood, Jr., "Intrinsic-Extrinsic Religious Orientation: The Boon or Bane of Contemporary Psychology of Religion?" *Journal for the Scientific Study of Religion* 29 (1990): 442-62.

54. Cf. Uri Bronfenbrenner, "Discovering What Families Do," in *Rebuilding the Nest: A New Commitment to the American Family*, ed. David Blankenhorn et al. (Milwaukee: Family Service America, 1990), p. 34. See also the research cited by Shirley Foster Hartley in *Illegitimacy* (Berkeley and Los Angeles: University of California Press, 1975), pp. 10-11.

cipients within five years of the birth of their first child. Sixty percent of mothers receiving AFDC (Aid for Families with Dependent Children) under the age of thirty had their first child during their teenage years.[55]

There are also direct negative consequences for the children born to teenage mothers. They are more likely to weigh less at birth and to have medical problems; the infant mortality rate for this group is higher, too. These children are also at greater risk for child abuse from immature mothers. They will have lower IQ rates and more behavior problems in school. Even when the parents of such children marry, they are more likely to have marital difficulties; there is a good chance that the marriage will not last. These problems are especially acute in the black community, where by 1980 nearly one out of ten black adolescent girls had a baby; 27 percent of this group had had at least one child previously.[56]

There is strong evidence that religion can help reduce the high rate of out-of-wedlock teenage pregnancies. The most comprehensive study of this problem, done at the Rand Corporation and published in 1988, tracked a nationally representative sample of high-school-sophomore women over two years. The authors of the study found that self-reported religiousness (response to the question "Do you think of yourself as a religious person?") was a strong predictor of subsequent single parenthood. As can be seen in Table 5.2, the highest rate of single parenthood was among those who pronounced themselves as not at all religious, while the lowest rate was among those who considered themselves very religious. Also, there was a markedly higher rate of out-of-wedlock pregnancy among those without a religious affiliation than among those affiliated with a church. Being black increased the chance of unmarried motherhood by several points, even after factors such as socioeconomic status and family background were taken into account. It appears that black girls undergo pubertal development and become sexually active earlier than their non-black counterparts, and that their social milieu is perceived as more accepting of out-of-wedlock birth.

55. The report is cited by Douglas J. Besharov, a resident scholar at the American Enterprise Institute, in his article entitled "Beyond Murphy Brown," *Washington Post*, 27 September 1992.

56. This is a summary of a longer discussion by Jewelle Taylor Gibbs, "Developing Intervention Models for Black Families: Linking Theory and Research," in *Black Families: Interdisciplinary Perspectives*, ed. Harold E. Cheatham and James B. Stewart (New Brunswick, N.J.: Transaction Books, 1990), pp. 332-33.

TABLE 5.2
Percentage Rates of Single Parenthood Sorted by Degree of Religiousness and Religious Affiliation

	Blacks	Hispanics	Whites
All Respondents	12.2%	5.0%	1.3%
Very religious	8.7	1.8	0.5
Somewhat religious	9.0	4.2	1.5
Not at all religious	19.7	4.6	1.5
No Religious Affiliation	18.0	10.3	1.8

Source: Allan F. Abrahamse, *Beyond Stereotypes* (1988)[57]

Since young women generally undergo religious development well before they are able to become pregnant, it is likely that what we see here is indeed a cause-and-effect relationship. Commenting on their findings, the authors of this study noted that the Christian religion proscribes childbearing outside of marriage and emphasizes marriage as the proper context for sexual activity, and so it stands to reason that those more faithful adherents would internalize these teachings more deeply. More religious individuals also tend to have traditional family-oriented values that would decrease the likelihood of their bearing a child out of wedlock. "Religiosity," the authors concluded, "may be a proxy for traditional or conservative values that discourage nontraditional family formation."[58] It is worth noting that even though the Roman Catholic Church opposes abortions and a high percentage of teenage pregnancies are ended by abortion, the rate of single parenthood was the same for white Catholic teens as for non-Catholics; for blacks and Hispanics, the rate was lower.

Several other studies have confirmed the importance of religiousness in promoting sexual abstinence. Studying 441 predominantly first-year and second-year college students, E. R. Mahoney found that the greater their religiousness, the less likely these students were to engage in premarital sexual activity. This finding held true for both male and female students.[59] Another study of young men and women,

57. Allan F. Abrahamse et al., *Beyond Stereotypes: Who Becomes a Single Teenage Mother?* (Santa Monica, Calif.: Rand Corporation, 1988), p. 38.
58. Ibid., p. 37.
59. Mahoney, "Religiosity and Sexual Behavior among Heterosexual College Students," *Journal of Sex Research* 16 (1980): 97-113.

done by Larry Jensen, confirmed the results of several earlier investigations, which showed that those who attended church every week had the lowest rate of premarital intercourse.[60] Not surprisingly, as an investigation published in 1991 showed, young people who are Pentecostals and Jehovah's Witnesses engage in less premarital sex than their nonreligious peers. High levels of religious commitment and social integration produced high levels of adherence to the principles of their religious faith.[61] The same holds true for American Muslims, among whom teenage pregnancies are said to be a rare phenomenon.[62]

The Mormon religion regards premarital sex as a grievous sin, and statistical data from the state of Utah, which is about 75 percent Mormon, reveal the important role that religion plays in influencing sexual conduct. Over the years, Utah has been consistently at or near the bottom of the scale for the number of births to teenage mothers. Utah also continues to have the lowest rate of out-of-wedlock births. In 1992, when the percentage of births to unmarried women was, on average, 28 for other states, it was 15 percent for Utah.[63] The difference undoubtedly would have been still greater were it not for the fact that Mormon doctrine regards routine resort to abortion as a sin comparable to murder; abortion rates in Utah are about one third the national average.[64]

Since the 1960s, many young Christians have become more permissive in their sexual attitudes (in conformity with broad cultural shifts). At the same time, research reveals that there continue to be lower rates of premarital sex and out-of-wedlock births among those with more rigorous religious beliefs. In the case of active Mormons,

60. Jensen et al., "Sexual Behavior, Church Attendance, and Permissive Beliefs among Unmarried Young Men and Women," *Journal for the Scientific Study of Religion* 29 (1990): 113-17.

61. Scott Beck et al., "Religious Heritage and Premarital Sex: Evidence from a National Sample of Young Adults," *Journal for the Scientific Study of Religion* 30 (1991): 177-80. It is worth recalling Alfred Kinsey's finding that religiously devout men and women participate less in all socially disapproved forms of sexual behavior; religion was the "most important factor in restricting premarital activity in the United States." See Kinsey et al., *Sexual Behavior in the Human Female* (Philadelphia: Saunders, 1953), pp. 324, 686-87.

62. Peter Steinfels, "Despite Role on World Stage, Muslims Turn to the Personal," *New York Times*, 7 May 1993.

63. U.S. Bureau of the Census, *Statistical Abstract of the United States: 1995*, Table 95, p. 77 (Washington, D.C.: Government Printing Office, 1995).

64. Ibid., Table 114, p. 84. See also Bruce A. Chadwick's "Teenage Pregnancy and Out-of-Wedlock Births," in *Utah in Demographic Perspective*, ed. Martin et al., pp. 27-28.

both males and females, we even find a slight trend toward more orthodox sexual behavior.[65]

In a book entitled *Religion May Be Hazardous to Your Health*, published in 1972, the psychiatrist Eli Chesen argued that fire-and-brimstone sermons about sex can lead to distorted views of human sexuality.[66] Such opinions notwithstanding, the consequences of premarital sex and out-of-wedlock births among teenagers, outlined earlier, would seem to lend weight to the conclusion that the sexual permissiveness condoned by many secularists represents a greater danger to the physical and psychological well-being of young people than the restrictive views of orthodox Christians.

Divorce

At first glance, divorce is not an action inviting moral judgment. Indeed, the legalization of divorce by mutual consent has often been hailed as a significant achievement of modern civilization. Divorce, writes social scientist William V. D'Antonio, expressing a rather typical viewpoint, "is the result of a core value, freedom, winning out over a less central traditional value, familism and group solidarity — and an even more abstract religious value, the sacredness of marriage."[67] And yet there is evidence to show that married people express a significantly greater degree of overall life satisfaction than divorced people and that children brought up by their biological parents in intact families are better off economically, emotionally, and developmentally than are children in other family structures. No doubt there are cases in which the dissolution of a marriage is the best thing for spouses and children. Instances of severe physical and psychological abuse do occur. Yet when the Christian religion came to teach the sacred status of the marriage bond, it may have been aware of something important after all.

A large number of studies have found a link between marital happiness and a sense of overall well-being. Allen Bergin has argued that

65. Cf. Darwin L. Thomas, "Family in the Mormon Experience," in *Families and Religions: Conflict and Change in Modern Society*, ed. William V. D'Antonio and Joan Aldous (Beverly Hills, Calif.: Sage, 1983), pp. 267-88.

66. Chesen, *Religion May Be Hazardous to Your Health* (New York: Peter H. Wyden, 1972), pp. 34-35.

67. D'Antonio, "Family Life, Religion, and Societal Values and Structures," in *Families and Religions*, ed. D'Antonio and Aldous, p. 98.

a good marriage and family life constitute a psychologically and socially benevolent state, while infidelity and disloyalty to an interpersonal commitment such as marriage lead to harmful consequences — both interpersonally and intrapsychically.[68] Several studies have shown that divorced people are much less optimistic than married people about whether life is worthwhile.[69] There is even stronger empirical evidence that children in disrupted families suffer serious negative consequences compared with children in intact families. Summarizing a large body of research, Richard Gill writes, "If one had to select the single most important factor responsible for the disturbing condition of many of today's younger generation . . . the breakdown of the intact biological-parent family would almost certainly be at or near the top of the list." Whether measured in economic terms or in terms of children's emotional development, behavior, psychological and physical well-being, and school performance, the data strongly support the superiority of the intact family and the high cost of divorce to children.[70]

This, then, is the context in which we must view the relationship of religiousness and divorce. The issue is not one of the validity of a religious doctrine. The consequences of divorce are real. All too often they involve a loss of happiness for one or both of the spouses as well as a lasting, damaging legacy for the children.

The steady increase in the breakup of families is long-term and worldwide. There are a number of reasons for this trend. A major one is the shift from an agrarian to an industrial and urban society, which has weakened links to the extended family and within the nuclear family. Also significant are the increased opportunities for and the acceptance of employment of women, which have given both women and men greater freedom to leave unhappy marriages. There is also modern society's stress on individualism, self-fulfillment, and personal satisfaction for both men and women. The upsurge in the divorce rate, notes one expert, "has been stimulated by a growing acceptance that divorce is a reasonable and, at times, even desirable alternative to an unhappy marriage."[71] In

68. Bergin, "Psychotherapy and Religious Values," *Journal of Consulting and Clinical Psychology* 48 (1980): 95-105.

69. Cf. Stan L. Albrecht et al., *Divorce and Remarriage: Problems, Adaptations, and Adjustments* (Westport, Conn.: Greenwood Press, 1983), p. 89.

70. Gill, "For the Sake of the Children," *Public Interest,* no. 108 (Summer 1992): 81-82. See also David Popenoe's *Disturbing the Nest: Family Change and Decline in Modern Societies* (New York: Aldine de Gruyter, 1988), p. 315.

71. Albrecht et al., *Divorce and Remarriage,* p. xi.

addition, the human potential movement, some varieties of feminism, and so-called progressive family social science have contributed to a weakening of the ideal of marital permanence. This in turn has caused a further downward trend in marital success. Realizing the low probability of success in marriage, Norval Glenn observes, people find it more difficult "to totally commit themselves to their marriages and to make the investment of time, effort, energy and forgone opportunities that a total commitment entails. And without such a commitment, marriages are unlikely to succeed."[72]

The United States has a higher divorce rate than other countries. What is called the crude divorce rate — the number of divorces and annulments per 1,000 population — increased in this country from 393 in 1960 to 1,166 in 1987.[73] During the 1980s, this striking increase in the number of marriage failures leveled off, and the number of children involved in divorce began to decrease. However, the fact remains that today approximately one half of all new marriages in the United States will end in divorce.

Numerous studies have shown a significant relationship between religiousness and marital adjustment and have indicated that religion operates as a powerful deterrent to divorce. In his pioneering sociological study of the Detroit area during the 1950s, Gerhard Lenski found that Catholics had a greater sense of family solidarity and a far lower divorce rate than Protestants. He surmised that since Catholic doctrine does not allow the dissolution of a consummated marriage, Catholics are under greater pressure than Protestants to make their marriages work.[74] James McCarthy confirmed this finding in a study published in 1979. Active Catholics were far less likely to separate than their Protestant counterparts; for Protestants, the probability of divorce increased substantially as religious commitment decreased. Conforming to powerful cultural trends in society as a whole, all groups of Christians showed increases in divorce, but the lowest rates continued to be among those who were actively religious.[75]

72. Glenn, "The Social and Cultural Meaning of Contemporary Marriage," in *The Retreat from Marriage: Causes and Consequences*, ed. Bryce Christensen (Lanham, Md.: University Press of America, 1990), p. 49.

73. U.S. Bureau of the Census, *Statistical Abstract of the United States: 1991* (Washington, D.C.: Government Printing Office, 1991), Table 128, p. 87.

74. Lenski, *The Religious Factor*, p. 219.

75. McCarthy, "Religious Commitment, Affiliation, and Marriage Dissolu-

The same results were reported by Stan Albrecht and his associates in their comprehensive investigation of divorce and remarriage published in 1983. Albrecht found a particularly strong relationship between divorce and two religious factors: not having had a church wedding and a low level of religious participation. While 10 percent of those who never attended church services were divorced, only 4 percent who attended services weekly experienced a breakup of their marriage.[76] The National Survey of Religious Identification undertaken at the City University of New York in 1989-90 revealed that those with no religious affiliation had the second-highest rate of divorce (after Unitarians).[77] A study by Margaret Wilson and Erik Filsinger published in 1986 revealed a strong positive relationship between several dimensions of religiousness and marital adjustment. The more conservative couples showed stronger family solidarity and a sharing of common interests.[78] A national marriage survey conducted by Gallup in 1988 revealed that 75 percent of those who prayed with their spouses (but only 57 percent of those who did not pray) reported that their marriages were very happy.[79] Other studies have shown a link between religious commitment, sexual ethics, and sexual satisfaction. Couples who were not involved sexually before marriage and who were faithful during their marriages are more satisfied with their current sex life than those who were involved sexually before marriage and/or engaged in extramarital affairs.[80]

If marital instability and divorce are seen as detrimental to both spouses and children — and the evidence for this conclusion is strong — then religiousness must be considered an important factor in reducing both. The old saying "The family that prays together stays together" no longer tells the entire story, but it does draw attention to the lasting significance of religiousness as a contributor to social stability. Many

---

tion," in *The Religious Dimension: New Directions in Quantitative Research*, ed. Robert Wuthnow (New York: Academic Press, 1979), pp. 188-94.

76. Albrecht et al., *Divorce and Remarriage*, pp. 51-53, 80-83.

77. Barry A. Kosmin, Director, *The National Survey of Religious Identification: 1989-90* (New York: City University of New York, 1991), p. 5.

78. Wilson and Filsinger, "Religiosity and Marital Adjustment: Multidimensional Interrelationships," *Journal of Marriage and the Family* 48 (1986): 147-51.

79. Andrew M. Greeley, *Faithful Attraction* (New York: Tor Books, 1991), discussed by David G. Myers in *The Pursuit of Happiness: Who Is Happy — and Why* (New York: William Morrow, 1992), p. 173.

80. This research is summarized by William R. Mattox, Jr., in "The Hottest Valentines," *Washington Post*, 13 February 1994.

Christians believe that there is no permanent commitment in marriage apart from the Christian faith itself, which stresses Jesus' injunction against putting asunder what God has joined together (Matt. 19:6). They regard marriage as a sacred bond rather than as a contractual arrangement to be terminated at the convenience of either party. Christian love is seen as resting on a firmer foundation than personal happiness or romantic involvement. Drawing on interviews with evangelical and other Christians, Robert Bellah summed up this perspective in this way:

> Of course, these Christians seek some of the same qualities of sharing, communication, and intimacy in marriage that define love for most Americans. But they are determined that these are goods to be sought within a framework of binding commitments, not the reasons for adhering to a commitment. Only by having an obligation to something higher than one's own preferences or one's own fulfillment, they insist, can one achieve a permanent love relationship.[81]

Available empirical evidence suggests that this attitude does work for large numbers of Americans. Once again, data about the Mormon church fill in the picture. In their 1983 study, Stan Albrecht and his associates reported that whereas 57 percent of Americans married in a civil setting were still in their first marriage, for the most committed members of the Mormon church (those married in a Mormon temple), the total was 87 percent.[82] Since Mormons are forbidden to divorce, one might think that such couples would tolerate unhappy marriages. One might surmise that the permanence of their marriages, enjoined by their religious creed, would be more important to them than their individual happiness. However, this hypothesis was tested in a study of 2,054 households in Utah, and it was unsubstantiated. Using three indicators of marital stability and happiness, Philip Kunz and Stan Albrecht found that 70.1 percent of those who attended church regularly expressed their willingness to marry the same partner again; for those who attended services only on special occasions or not at all, the corresponding percentages were 55.0 and 53.7 percent respectively. Regular churchgoers also reported substantially fewer disagreements in their marriages. The researchers concluded that religiousness was strongly associated with several measures of marital

---

81. Bellah et al., *Habits of the Heart: Individualism and Commitment in American Life* (New York: Harper & Row, 1986), p. 97.
82. Albrecht et al., *Divorce and Remarriage*, p. 80.

happiness: "Sharing a common interest through religious participation
. . . does seem to have an important effect on marital satisfaction."[83]

The state of Utah, it should be readily conceded, is not paradise on
earth. Its population is buffeted by the same powerful winds of change
that beset the rest of America. Moreover, even strong adherence to the
Mormon religion is certainly not tantamount to moral perfection, for
Mormons are human like the rest of us. These individuals are able to
avoid certain kinds of undesirable conduct, but a more complete picture
of their lives might bring to light other, less positive characteristics.[84] I
should also emphasize that none of the findings discussed here suggest
that religion is the only factor in the highly complex moral crisis of modern
society; nevertheless, these findings do indicate that religiousness can be
a powerful determinant moderating this crisis.

Conclusion

As I indicated at the beginning of this chapter, most religious thinkers
disclaim any link between adherence to the Christian faith and superior
moral conduct. But the available social-scientific research surveyed here
contradicts this modesty. It shows that the minority of Christians who
take their religion seriously are different from nominal members of the
Christian churches. Whether it be juvenile delinquency, adult crime,
prejudice, out-of-wedlock births, or marital conflict and divorce, there
is a significantly lower rate of such indicators of moral failure and
social ills among believing Christians. The vast majority of the research
available supports this finding; only an occasional study is either in-
conclusive or points in another direction.

Some of the research that has failed to corroborate the constructive role of religion is so obviously biased that it can be ignored. Take
Milton Rokeach's report in 1969 that religious individuals showed less

83. Kunz and Albrecht, "Religion, Marital Happiness and Divorce," *International Journal of Sociology of the Family* 7 (1977): 230.
84. In his book entitled *The Darker Side of Virtue: Corruption, Scandal,
and the Mormon Empire* (Buffalo, N.Y.: Prometheus, 1991), sociologist Anson
Shupe challenges the moral reputation of the Mormon population of Utah, but his
evidence consists of no more than several isolated, albeit widely publicized, instances of individual wrongdoing likely to be found in any large population.
Whatever the moral shortcomings of the Mormons, it would appear that their
conduct is less overtly antisocial — it does not cause as much harm or impose as
many burdens on society as does the behavior of less religious individuals.

social compassion than other Americans.[85] Since his criteria of "social compassion" included measures such as support for a guaranteed annual income and sympathy with the student-protest movement, this conclusion was, of course, hardly unexpected. Conservative Christians rejected these things not because they lacked compassion but because they did not share the liberal approach to social problems exemplified by Rokeach's criteria.[86] More meaningful indicators of compassion would seem to be the findings of more recent studies that 38 percent of the most religious Americans did volunteer work for a local organization, while only 6 percent of the least religious showed such involvement in their communities, and the fact that those who every week attend a church or a synagogue are two and a half times more generous in giving to charity than those who never attend religious services.[87] Or again, it is well known that the religiousness of parents correlates highly with their willingness to care for a child with disabilities,[88] and such conduct, too, appears to be a more valid measure of compassion than a respondent's position on certain ideologically charged issues of the day.

Several caveats are necessary in order to assess correctly the significance of the empirical findings discussed in this chapter. First, while the studies examined show clearly that religiousness is related to various important forms of human conduct, few of them tell us anything about causative effects. In order to establish conclusively that religiousness *causes* people to be better, one would need longitudinal studies that follow the lives of individuals over a significant period of time; in this way the appearance of various results could be observed and recorded. But relatively little research into human behavior conforms to this model, and without such conformity, observed relationships may hide true causes. For example, the fact that there is a high

---

85. Rokeach, "Religious Values and Social Compassion," *Review of Religious Research* 11 (1969): 24-39.

86. This point is well made by one of his critics, Richard L. Gorsuch, in "Rokeach's Approach to Value Systems and Social Compassion," *Review of Religious Research* 11 (1969): 139-43.

87. See *The Connecticut Mutual Life Report on American Values in the 1980s: The Impact of Belief* (New York: Research and Forecasts, 1981), p. 66. Similar findings are reported by Gallup and Jones in *The Saints among Us*, p. 69, and by Robert Wuthnow in *Acts of Compassion: Caring for Others and Helping Ourselves* (Princeton, N.J.: Princeton University Press, 1991), p. 125.

88. See, for example, G. H. Zuk's article entitled "The Religious Factor and Role of Guilt in Parental Acceptance of the Retarded Child," *American Journal of Mental Deficiencies* 64 (1959): 145-53.

correlation between the number of fire engines at a fire and the amount of damage done by the blaze does not establish that one causes the other. In fact, each is caused by a hidden variable — the size of the fire. In the same way, it is possible that an observed relationship between religiousness and moral conduct may be spurious and may obscure a truly causative factor. Perhaps it is the case that deviant behavior, whatever its cause, leads people to neglect their religious activities and weakens their religious convictions rather than that religiousness inhibits deviance.[89]

Second, little research in the social sciences is cumulative and conclusive. The scales or criteria used may not be fully comparable; these dissimilarities will often disallow generalization to a larger population. In some situations, religiousness will be effective only in combination with another variable, and it may not be possible to determine which of the two is the more important. For example, we know that, especially for young people, family and peer influences are highly significant; these factors may make it difficult to isolate the impact of the religious factor.[90]

And yet, even after these caveats have been taken into account, the empirical research examined leaves us with some important insights. It is not unimportant to establish that there exists a significant relationship between religiousness and the observance of certain moral and social norms. In time, we may be able to find explanations for the relationship. It may be that worship and the feeling of being loved by God indeed produce definite changes in a person's behavior. Such a person may not develop a need for drugs, succumb to extramarital affairs, and so on. Or it may be, as suggested by cognitive consistency theories of psychology, that regular participation in worship where sermons are preached keeps reminding people of their ideals. In turn, the need for people to see their conduct as consistent with their ideals may provide support for the maintenance of moral norms.[91]

89. Cf. Charles R. Tittle and Michael R. Welch, "Religiosity and Deviance: Towards a Contingency Theory of Constraining Effects," *Social Forces* 61 (1983): 656.

90. Kirk Elifson et al., "Religiosity and Delinquency," *Criminology* 21 (1983): 521.

91. Cf. the careful discussion by Richard L. Gorsuch, "Religion as a Significance Predictor of Important Human Behavior," in *Research in Mental Health and Religious Behavior,* ed. William J. Donaldson (Atlanta, Ga.: Psychological Studies Institute, 1976), p. 21.

Even in the absence of fully explanatory models, modern statistical techniques enable us to predict, for example, what kinds of adolescents are more likely to become involved in illicit drug use or have a child out of wedlock. Since the development of religious faith usually predates experimentation with drugs and sex, we have some indication of cause and effect even if we do not fully understand the specific psychological mechanisms involved. Such findings may have important implications for policy. Lastly, the ongoing work of the churches in dealing with various social disorders provides additional information about what works and what does not work. We will look at some of this information in more detail in the final chapter.

6. The Need for Religiousness

Some of the most serious social problems confronting America today, as I argued in an earlier chapter, involve patterns of personal behavior, defects of character, and, most basically, cultural trends that have undermined traditional values. The sharp rise in youth violence — especially the brutality with which many of these crimes are carried out — is a powerful reminder that the crisis we confront is at bottom a moral crisis. In our inner cities, guns and gunfights have become routine ways of settling disputes between young people — disputes over whether someone looked at someone else the wrong way or stepped on somebody's foot. Others kill because they want someone's fashionable item of clothing or, unbelievably enough, because it's something they feel like doing: in a 1992 incident in the nation's capital, one teen shot another because he "felt like shooting someone." Recently, two seventeen-year-olds in New York City lured another teenager to an abandoned building, bound his hands, and threw him down an elevator shaft. To make sure that their victim was dead, they dropped heavy metal objects down the shaft, crushing his skull. A few days before he was killed, the mildly retarded boy had complained to his mother that his "friends" were beating him on a weekly basis and taking his money.[1] In another incident, four teenagers in New York City set fire to a homeless man sleeping on a bench in a subway station. According to the transit police, between January and April 1992, fourteen other homeless people had been set afire, and several of them died from their

1. Craig Wolff, "Two Teen-Agers Charged in Elevator-Shaft Death," *New York Times*, 26 October 1992.

injuries.[2] Unfortunately, these are not isolated horror stories but regularly occurring events marked by a total failure of conscience and disregard for the value of life.

The typical elementary-school child spends thirty hours a week watching television. It is estimated that by the age of eighteen, the average child will have witnessed 10,000 killings on the screen. "Is it any wonder," asked psychiatrist-columnist Charles Krauthammer in a recent article entitled "Culture Has Consequences," "that a growing number might like to commit just one? Sexual aggression and misogyny are celebrated in rap. Is it any wonder that kids arrested for rape and murder are utterly conscienceless and uncomprehending?"[3] Social scientists continue to argue over whether there is a proven relationship between crime and children's exposure to violence through the media. A majority of researchers today believe that television violence contributes to undesirable, antisocial behavior,[4] but a vocal minority dispute this conclusion. Meanwhile, the mayhem in the streets continues, especially in the nation's black ghettos.

Between 1987 and 1991, the rate of violent crime — robbery, rape, aggravated assault, and murder — rose 29 percent overall and 24 percent in per-capita terms; killings carried out by teenagers have increased sharply. Gang membership and fights with other gangs offer teenagers what many of them have not gotten at home or elsewhere: a sense of family, rules to live by, power, and respect. While the overall rate of violent crime has declined since 1991, between 1985 and 1993 weapons-related arrests of juveniles more than doubled, and from 1985 to 1991 homicide among young men between the ages of fifteen and nineteen increased by 97 percent; homicide now is the leading cause of death for black men between the ages of fifteen and thirty-four.[5] The

2. "Youths Set Homeless Man Afire in Subway," *New York Times*, 5 October 1992.

3. Krauthammer, "Culture Has Consequences," *Washington Post*, 26 October 1990.

4. Cf. George Comstock, *Television in America*, 2nd ed. (Newbury Park, Calif.: Sage, 1991), pp. 121-24. See also Brandon S. Centerwall's "Television and Violent Crime," *Public Interest*, no. 111 (Spring 1993): 56-71; and Edward Donnerstein's and Daniel Linz's essay entitled "The Media," in *Crime*, ed. James Q. Wilson and Joan Petersilia (San Francisco: ICS Press, 1995), pp. 237-64.

5. U.S. Bureau of the Census, *Statistical Abstract of the United States: 1993* (Washington, D.C.: Government Printing Office, 1993), Table 300, p. 192, and Table 134, p. 98; Neil A. Lewis, "Crime: Falling Rates But Rising Fear," *New York Times*, 8 December 1993; Fox Butterfield, "Teen-age Homicide Rate Has Soared,"

upsurge of inner-city violence is fueled by the crack epidemic and the disintegration of normal social life in many urban neighborhoods. The inner cities have lost mediating structures such as churches, neighborhood stores, voluntary organizations, and ordinary street life that once formed a buffer between criminals and law-abiding citizens.[6]

In an age of mass culture that frequently emphasizes self-fulfillment at the expense of values and that reaches into every home, large numbers of young people, black and white, grow up stunted in their moral development. A survey conducted by the Rhode Island Rape Crisis Center in 1988 asked 1,700 pupils in grades six to nine, "Is it acceptable for a man to force a woman to have sex if he has spent money on her?" A total of 24 percent of the boys and 16 percent of the girls in grades seven to nine answered "yes." When asked, "Is it acceptable for a man to force a woman to have sex if they have been dating for more than six months?" 65 percent of the boys and 47 percent of the girls responded in the affirmative. Educators speak of "ethical illiteracy."[7]

The root cause of failure here is the crisis of the family, for it is the home that has the greatest influence upon a child's moral development. That is the place where a child learns morality — both values that are taught and, more important, values that are implicitly assumed and expressed in personal relationships between parents and child. There is abundant evidence that a child brought up in a loving home atmosphere and with firm, but not arbitrary, discipline has the best chance of developing into a well-balanced, secure, and generous person. In many instances today, the home no longer fulfills the crucial function of transmitting constructive and moral ways to behave. Large numbers of children grow up without fathers able to serve as role models. Many single mothers are themselves still children and therefore are unable to inculcate mature habits of conduct in their offspring.

"The family," well-known social analyst Michael Novak has written, "is nature's original department of health, education and human

---

New York Times, 14 October 1994; "Weapons Offenses Up among Young, Study Says," *New York Times*, 13 November 1995.

6. Cf. William Tucker, "Is Police Brutality the Problem?" *Commentary*, January 1993, p. 25.

7. The survey results are reported by Thomas Lickona in *Educating for Character: How Our Schools Can Teach Respect and Responsibility* (New York: Bantam Books, 1992), p. 5.

services."[8] When things go well in the family, all of society benefits. When the family fails, other social institutions have a very difficult time picking up the pieces. There is no easy way to compensate for the inability of many parents to tend to the moral needs of their children. Neither can broad cultural trends be changed by edict or denunciation. At the same time, institutions such as schools and churches can exert an influence upon the moral development of children. This influence may not be able to make up for all the failings of the home, but it can provide a limited way of halting moral disarray.

The Importance of Moral Education

During the nineteenth century, it was taken for granted that the public schools had some responsibility for teaching virtue and character. According to Horace Mann, "the father of American public education," American society could not flourish and remain free without a strong emphasis on moral education, and the foundation of morality was religion. Protestant thinkers in particular stressed the link between the Christian religion and sound morals; the view that religion was indispensable to the social health of a free country inevitably meant bringing religious values into the schoolroom. What we now call "Victorian morality" involved an emphasis on the importance of self-control as well as an emphasis on the values of patriotism, hard work, honesty, altruism, and courage. Children practiced reading by using the *McGuffey Reader*, which provided them with tales of heroism and virtue. The power of stirring stories to pass on traditional wisdom is, of course, well known. Such literature opens our hearts and minds and enriches our moral imagination. Heroes and heroines who triumph over adversity inspire us with their example and strengthen our determination to do good despite the cost. As Iris Murdoch, the English philosopher, has put it, "Art transcends selfish and obsessive limitations of personality and can enlarge the sensibility of its consumer. It is a kind of goodness by proxy. Most of all it exhibits to us the connection in human beings of clear realistic vision with compassion."[9]

8. Novak et al., *A Community of Self-Reliance: The New Consensus on Family and Welfare* (Washington, D.C.: American Enterprise Institute, 1987), p. 16.
9. Murdoch, *The Sovereignty of Good* (New York: Schocken Books, 1971), p. 87. See also the excellent discussion by Sidney Callahan entitled *In Good Con-*

It is significant that the second half of the nineteenth century and the first part of the twentieth saw a decline in reported crime in America despite rapid industrialization, urbanization, a large influx of immigrants, and a widening of the divisions between classes.[10] The reduction in the crime rate was helped by successful efforts to reduce alcohol consumption and to proclaim the virtues of honest work and the evils of idleness — efforts aimed at building character, especially in young people. During the 1920s and 1930s, the teaching of morality came under attack as a violation of "scientific thinking," then in vogue. Nevertheless, the public schools continued to affirm, at least tacitly, "the American way of life" — what sociologist Will Herberg called the operative public religion and central spiritual structure of American society.[11] By the 1960s, this common faith had lost much of its luster, and the phrase "Victorian morality" had come to be used with condescension. The defiance of impulse control was now celebrated as "cool" and commendable. The modern ethic of self-expression and self-fulfillment had taken the place of self-control. A tendency to rank personal gratification above obligation to others, Robert Bellah noted, was accompanied by "a deepening cynicism about the established social, economic, and political institutions of society."[12] The new emphasis on individual freedom brought with it concern for the rights of women and children and encouraged new ideas in art, literature, and politics; the civil rights movement was one of its benefits. However, the new individualism also gave rise to a rebellion against tradition. In the schools, it led to a reluctance on the part of teachers to assert their authority and to a shallow moral relativism and the introduction of values clarification, which regarded moral education as indoctrination. Education no longer included passing on the basic values of our culture.

By the mid-1970s, the pendulum had swung back. Since then, in response to the increase in violence and drug use, many schools have reintroduced dress codes and rules of civil behavior. It is estimated

science: Reason and Emotion in Moral Decision Making (New York: HarperCollins, 1991), pp. 206-8.

10. Cf. James Q. Wilson, "The Rediscovery of Character: Private Virtue and Public Policy," *Public Interest,* no. 81 (Fall 1985): 12.

11. Herberg, *Protestant-Catholic-Jew: An Essay in American Religious Sociology* (Garden City, N.Y.: Doubleday, 1955).

12. Bellah, *The Broken Covenant: Civil Religion in Time of Trial* (New York: Seabury Press, 1975), p. x.

that about one in five public-school districts now offer formal programs in moral education, ranging from occasional classes in ethics to more ambitious and overarching programs.[13] These courses reaffirm and teach the values of our heritage, about which there is general agreement. As Thomas Lickona, a psychologist and professor of education, puts it, "We don't want them [children] to lie, cheat on tests, take what's not theirs, call names, hit each other, or be cruel to animals; we do want them to tell the truth, play fair, be polite, respect their parents and teachers, do their school work, and be kind to others."[14] The influential educational theorist Lawrence Kohlberg, who at one time rejected the idea of teaching a specific set of virtues, eventually came to recognize the importance of value content in moral education.[15]

Several private groups have developed curricula for moral education. One of the first such efforts was undertaken by the American Institute for Character Education in San Antonio, Texas (now called the Character Education Institute). As of October 1991, this curriculum, covering character education from kindergarten through ninth grade, was in use in more than 50,000 classrooms in over forty-five states. It encourages the values of honesty, truthfulness, tolerance, generosity, kindness, and helpfulness. In October 1993, Barbara Jordan, the former Congresswoman from Texas, and actor Tom Selleck announced the formation of the Character Counts Coalition, a consortium of twenty-seven organizations seeking to promote moral education in the schools.[16] Most such programs have not been subjected to a controlled research evaluation, but the empirical studies that have been done, as well as reports made by teachers and principals, indicate improvement in self-esteem among students and a decline in truancy and other disciplinary problems. A survey done by the Gallup organization in 1992 showed that teenagers urged by their schools to do voluntary community work were

13. Kimberly J. McLarin, "Curriculum or Not, Teachers Teach Values," *New York Times*, 1 February 1995.

14. Lickona, *Educating for Character*, p. 47. See also Suzanne Daley's article entitled "Pendulum Is Swinging Back to the Teaching of Values in U.S. Schools," *New York Times*, 12 December 1990.

15. Cf. Barry I. Chazan, *Contemporary Approaches to Moral Education* (New York: Teachers College Press, 1985), p. 82.

16. Nadine Brozan, "Chronicle," *New York Times*, 8 October 1993. A list of organizations promoting character education is provided by Amitai Etzioni in "Schools and the Subject of Character," *Washington Post Education Review*, 3 April 1994.

almost twice as likely to volunteer for such activities than students from schools that did not promote altruism.[17]

The return of moral education has been welcomed by many communities, but it has also met with resistance from teachers still enamored of the ways of the 1960s. Some of them express opposition to foisting white, middle-class values on what they say are multicultural classes. When abandoned as a formal program, values clarification often survives in classes on drug education, sex education, and life skills. In the face of opposition from teachers, several states have had to abandon the introduction of moral education.[18] Some opponents of moral education in the public schools have expressed fears that the teaching of the moral legacy of Judeo-Christian culture will undermine the separation of church and state. This concern is unwarranted. Public schools cannot and should not promote a particular religion, but they can and should accurately portray the role of religion in history (which is not something they now do). By omitting the subject, public schools in effect teach that religion is of no importance; such a policy also ignores the fact that for the large majority of Americans, religion and morality are inseparable. The schools should teach values that compel universal consent because they are part of our common heritage, not because they are part of a particular religious tradition. At the same time, there is nothing wrong with teachers pointing out the contribution that religion has made to the development of this moral heritage.

To bring emphases on character and ethics back into the schools would involve more than changes in the curriculum; it would require a total ethos that would stress a positive moral environment and the promotion of habits of proper conduct. As Aristotle recognized more than two thousand years ago, a good character is achieved through the development of good habits. "An effective moral education," argues William Kilpatrick in his insightful book entitled *Why Johnny Can't Tell Right from Wrong*, "would be devoted to encouraging habits of honesty, helpfulness and self-control until such behavior becomes second nature."[19]

The long-term success of instruction in values will depend on shaking up the educational establishment. Furthermore, moral education

17. Liz Spayd, "Study Shows Increase in Teen Voluntarism," *Washington Post*, 4 December 1992.
18. Sonia L. Nazario, "Teachers Say It's Wrongheaded to Try to Teach Students What's Right," *Wall Street Journal*, 6 April 1990.
19. Kilpatrick, *Why Johnny Can't Tell Right from Wrong* (New York: Simon & Schuster, 1992), p. 97.

will become generally accepted only if Americans finally realize the high cost of what passes for value neutrality. Many parents in our inner cities, disturbed by the lack of discipline and the low quality of education in their schools, now send their children to religious institutions that work to instill in students the values which the public schools have come to disregard.[20] Between 1970 and 1990, non-Catholic enrollment in Catholic schools rose from 2.6 to 14.3 percent. The percentage of Hispanics in Catholic secondary schools now exceeds that in the public sector.[21] In addition to enhanced academic achievement, one of the main attractions of these schools is their emphasis on character building, a strong commitment to the basic values of truthfulness, justice, and human compassion.

The Role of the Churches and Personal Discipline

The founders of the American republic were keenly aware of the role that religious beliefs play in restraining human passions and naked self-interest. "Whatever may be conceded to the influence of refined education on minds of peculiar structure," George Washington wrote in his farewell address, "reason and experience both forbid us to expect that national morality can prevail in exclusion of religious principle."[22]

Since these lines were written in 1796, this insight has lost none of its validity, but religious institutions have not always lived up to the task of inculcating morality. Today, many mainline churches in particular fail to do justice to this important assignment. At a time when large majorities of Americans are members of churches and affirm their belief in God, survey research reveals that the great majority of church members hold values that are in no way distinctive. Religion plays a crucial role in the formation of character and the teaching of virtue, yet many of the clergy neglect to speak normatively about family values and other basic moral issues. There is a strong tendency, as one recent observer has put it, "to worship a God who, far from judging believers or even challenging them to seek a more virtuous life, tends to massage them, reinforcing them in whatever they have already chosen to do

20. Michael Abramowitz, "Educational Haven in Inner-City Chicago," *Washington Post,* 17 October 1992.

21. Anthony S. Bryk et al., *Catholic Schools and the Common Good* (Cambridge, Mass.: Harvard University Press, 1993), p. 69.

22. George Washington, *The Farewell Address: The View from the Twentieth Century,* ed. Burton Ira Kaufman (Chicago: Quadrangle Books, 1969), pp. 24-25.

anyway."[23] Most Christians have what Gordon Allport called an extrinsic rather than an intrinsic religious outlook: religion is not integral to their personal lives but something that they find useful and reassuring. A recent study that applied a twelve-item scale of religiousness concluded that the number of "everyday saints" who truly live what they profess amounts to no more than 13 percent of the U.S. adult population or about 17 percent of those who consider themselves Christians.[24] Those who do internalize the key values of their faith are the ones whose personal conduct shows a distinctly different pattern. As we saw in an earlier chapter, whether it be juvenile delinquency, prejudice, out-of-wedlock births, or marital conflict and divorce, there is a significantly lower rate of such indicators of moral failure and social ills among the minority of Christians who take their religion seriously. Without over-stating the significance of these empirical findings, it is clear that true religiousness can be a force that moderates the crisis of modernity and wards off some of its deleterious effects.

The contribution of the churches in countering the moral disarray of modern society is of special importance in the African-American community, where, as we have seen, the crisis of the family plays such a crucial role in the growth of the underclass in our cities. The black churches are well positioned to play a constructive role in the life of their communities, because there is a high rate of religious participation among blacks. There are over 75,000 black churches in America, and 70 percent of black adults belong to one of these churches.[25] Eighty-seven percent of blacks (compared with 56 percent of whites) consider religion "very important" in their lives.[26]

23. William J. Gould, Jr., "The Challenge of Liberal Political Culture in the Thought of John Courtney Murray," paper presented at a seminar at the American Enterprise Institute on 1 October 1992.

24. The figure of 13 percent (24 million of the U.S. adult population) is given by George H. Gallup, Jr., and Timothy Jones in *The Saints among Us* (Harrisburg, Pa.: Morehouse, 1992), pp. 13, 15. Twenty-four million "saints" represent about 17 percent of all those who consider themselves Christians. Using a somewhat different scale of religious commitment, another group of researchers has found that the percentage of adult Americans whose religion informs their attitudes or behavior is about 19 percent. Cf. Lyman A. Kellstedt et al., "Religious Traditions and Religious Commitments in the USA," unpublished paper delivered at the 22nd International Conference of the International Society of Religion, Budapest, Hungary, 19-23 July 1993.

25. Andrew Billingsley, *Climbing Jacob's Ladder: The Enduring Legacy of African-American Families* (New York: Simon & Schuster, 1992), pp. 73, 353.

26. George Gallup, Jr., and Robert Bezilla, "More Find Religion Important," *Washington Post*, 22 January 1994.

The black churches of America represent the oldest social institution in African-American history, and they have long been involved in promoting education and moral uplift. They have also helped create a tradition of self-help and self-reliance in the black community. During the period of Reconstruction, when large numbers of freed slaves were suddenly on their own without resources, the black churches cultivated the virtues and values of industry, thrift, sobriety, discipline, and the postponement of immediate gratification. Many black leaders, especially Booker T. Washington, saw the cultivation of morality and economic advancement as the major means of black acceptance in American society. W. E. B. Du Bois, who stressed the importance of adult education, also saw the involvement of the church as a key to the task of strengthening black families.[27] The emphasis on self-help was consistent with the dominant way of thinking about poverty in the nineteenth century, which stressed the crucial importance of religion in building character and a sense of empowerment. In a statement typical of this era, Charles Loring Brace (founder of the New York Children's Aid Society) argued, "Christianity is the highest education of character. Give the poor that, and only seldom will either alms or punishment be necessary."[28] During the nineteenth century, the great potential of this philosophy was proven by the mission movement in America's urban slums as well as by the black churches.

By stressing the values of hard work and discipline, many black churches have succeeded in creating an ethos of upward mobility among their members. A case in point is the Church of God in Christ, the largest black Pentecostal denomination, established by Bishop Charles H. Mason in the early twentieth century. In the beginning, the vast majority of its members were illiterate, poor, rural migrants in urban centers. They met in storefront churches and were often scorned or ridiculed because of their ecstatic worship, their practice of speaking in tongues, and their lower-class background. As recently as

---

27. Cf. C. Eric Lincoln and Lawrence H. Mamiya, *The Black Church in the African-American Experience* (Durham, N.C.: Duke University Press, 1990), p. 243; and Thomas G. Poole, "Black Families and the Black Church: A Sociohistorical Perspective," in *Black Families: Interdisciplinary Perspectives*, ed. Harold E. Cheatham and James B. Stewart (New Brunswick, N.J.: Transaction, 1990), p. 39.

28. Brace, *The Dangerous Classes of New York and Twenty Years' Work among Them* (New York: Wynkoop and Hallenbeck, 1880), pp. 22-23, quoted by Marvin N. Olasky in *The Tragedy of American Compassion* (Washington, D.C.: Regnery Gateway, 1992), p. 35.

1926, the Church of God in Christ had no more than 30,000 members; however, because it was the fastest-growing black denomination, it became impressively large over the years: by 1983 it had a membership of 3.7 million. Many of these members were now attaining working-class or middle-income status, and the storefront churches that had once characterized the denomination were fast disappearing. Increasingly, worship now takes place in regular church buildings.[29]

The Church of God in Christ is not the only black denomination to have undergone changes in its class composition. Also now predominantly middle class are the African Methodist Episcopal Church, with 2.2 million members; the African Methodist Episcopal Zion Church, with 1.2 million members; the Christian Methodist Episcopal Church, with 900,000 members; and some black Baptist churches. There is also the well-known phenomenon of the Black Muslims, who have achieved rigorously high moral standards for both personal and group behavior.[30]

The important role that religion can play in fostering upward mobility is confirmed by a 1986 study carried out by Richard Freeman, director of the labor statistics program at the National Bureau of Economic Research and professor of economics at Harvard University. It showed that among male black youths, churchgoing was a good predictor of success in escaping inner-city poverty. Those who attended church had a higher rate of school attendance or employment and a lower rate of deviant behavior. "Although it is difficult to determine the causal links by which churchgoing affects behavior," Freeman conceded, "the pattern of statistical results suggests that at least some part of the churchgoing effect is the result of an actual causal impact."[31] Interpreting these findings, Eric Lincoln and Lawrence Mamiya suggested that churchgoing reduced the social isolation of inner-city youths and put them in contact with the role models of working adults. It also exposed them to the self-help tradition of black churches. "The successful internalization of the values of the black self-help tradition

29. Lincoln and Mamiya, *The Black Church in the African-American Experience*, p. 335.

30. C. Eric Lincoln, *The Black Muslims in America* (Boston: Beacon Press, 1961), p. 67.

31. Freeman, "Who Escapes? The Relation of Churchgoing and Other Background Factors to the Socioeconomic Performance of Black Male Youths from Inner-City Tracts," in *The Black Youth Employment Crisis*, ed. Richard B. Freeman and Harry J. Holzer (Chicago: University of Chicago Press, 1986), pp. 372-73.

is dependent upon a socializing environment that will continually reinforce and reaffirm those values in a caring way," concluded Lincoln and Mamiya.[32] Lastly, there is the finding of the 1988 Rand Corporation study, discussed earlier in this book, that religious identification can help reduce the high rate of out-of-wedlock births among young black women who live in the inner city.

How are these black churches attacking the problems of the inner city and of the black family? A consortium of ten churches in Chicago has developed a program, Project IMAGE, which seeks to strengthen the image, role, and presence of black males in families, churches, schools, and communities. With grants from the Ford and Lilly foundations, the Congress of National Black Churches has set up a program called Project Spirit, which provides training for the clergy of inner-city churches to make them more effective pastoral counselors in dealing with issues such as parent-child communication, sexuality, and teen pregnancy. A similar program, called Black Manhood Training: Body, Mind and Soul, was developed at the University of Virginia and is being used in several southern black churches to train deacons in youth counseling. Some churches set up housing corporations, rehabilitate neighborhood stores, and run their own schools.[33] In October 1993, the Reverend Jesse Jackson announced a program under which black churches in New York City would be asked to distribute pledge cards to parishioners with children: parents would promise to take their children to school, meet their teachers, read their children's report cards, and turn off their television sets at home for at least three hours every night. "Around the country," Jackson declared, "there is this rage of violence, not born of poverty and neglect as much as driven by drugs and guns and perverse values."[34]

Black churches of course use the pulpit as well as formal programs in an attempt to instill biblical values, though the results appear to be disappointing in some respects. The main problem here is how to reach the inner-city underclass, especially young adults. Most members of black churches are working class or middle class. For the first time in black history, write Lincoln and Mamiya, an unchurched

32. Lincoln and Mamiya, *The Black Church in the African-American Experience*, p. 335.

33. Ibid., pp. 257-58, 339. Another description of outreach activities by black churches is given by Billingsley in *Climbing Jacob's Ladder*, pp. 357-71.

34. Quoted by Ronald Sullivan in "Jackson Plan to Reduce School Rage," *New York Times*, 12 October 1993.

generation of young black people is growing up in urban areas without knowledge of, interest in, or respect for religion. The street culture brands participation in religious activities as "straight" or as the province of older black women.[35] In other words, those who are most in need of the socializing influence of religion are largely beyond the sway of the black churches.

One of those troubled by the failure of traditional remedies is Keith Butler, pastor of the Word of Faith Christian Center in Detroit and chairman of the Coalition for the Restoration of the Black Family and Society, founded in 1991. Butler stresses the crucial importance of self-help and a strong work ethic in order to overcome welfare dependency.[36] A similar position is taken by Steve Gooden, pastor of the Granada Hills Community Church in Los Angeles. However, the clergy who call upon people to take charge of their own lives are often overshadowed by those who proclaim the overriding importance of white racism, attribute all problems to the victimization of blacks, and demand more government help in order to prevent the fire next time. Al Sharpton of Brooklyn is the best known of these clergymen, who tend to gain the attention of the media. Richard Neuhaus has commented pointedly on this situation: "The preachers of self-reliance and moral reconstruction are declared to be 'conservative,' the ultimate epithet of liberal dismissiveness. In truth, they are the real reformers who are challenging the status quo that is supported by a civil rights establishment and welfare bureaucracy that, some good intentions notwithstanding, encourage the perpetual infantilizing of the inner-city poor."[37]

What the population of the inner cities needs, Irving Kristol has argued, is a black John Wesley who could do for the "underclass in the ghettos what Wesley did for the gin-ridden, loose-living working class in eighteenth-century Britain."[38] The suggestion is apt, for the charismatic founder of Methodism indeed was successful in instilling a sense of personal responsibility in many of the miners and factory workers of England's growing industrial centers. Wesley preached that salvation

35. Lincoln and Mamiya, *The Black Church in the African-American Experience*, pp. 310-22.

36. See Steve Beard, "Pastor Keith Butler: Motor-Town Councilman," *Charisma*, June 1992, p. 18.

37. Editorial, "What Should We Do about the Poor?" *First Things*, April 1992, p. 9.

38. Kristol, "Skepticism, Meliorism, and the Public Interest," *Public Interest*, no. 81 (Fall 1985): 39.

was dependent upon the individual's responsible behavior. "I exhorted the little society," Wesley recorded in 1765, "to avoid sloth, prodigality, and sluttishness, and, on the contrary, to be patterns of diligence, frugality, and cleanliness."[39] Honesty, chastity, and sobriety were normative, with violators subject to expulsion from the community of the faithful. Discipline was to enable the poor and degraded to attain virtue and live like children of God. Those who were reached by this appeal underwent a spiritual transformation and became changed individuals. Through hard work and with the aid of various self-help organizations, Methodists set about to improve their social condition, and became increasingly prosperous.[40]

In a similar vein, Robert Woodson, founder and president of the National Center for Neighborhood Enterprise, has emphasized the point that social programs, while important, by themselves will not make a difference. These things "have no redemptive quality, and what our young people need above all is to be redeemed":

> The people whose work I know at firsthand — people like Sister Fatah, who has turned gang members around in Philadelphia; Charles Ballard, who has led hundreds of single fathers in Cleveland to accept responsibility for their children and, in many cases, to marry the mothers of those children; Freddie Garcia, who was a drug addict and thief for 15 years before he 'came to himself' and started a highly successful drug rehabilitation program in San Antonio — all these people have two things in common. First, they share zip codes with the people they serve, and second, they call these young people unto themselves, connect at a spiritual level, tell them they have got to change their ways.[41]

It probably is true, as Chester Finn has put it, that current inner-city antisocial behavior bespeaks "impoverishment more of the

---

39. Wesley, *The Journal of John Wesley* (London: Epworth Press, 1909-16), V:118, quoted by Bernard Semmel in *The Methodist Revolution* (New York: Basic Books, 1973), p. 73.

40. Maldwyn Edwards, *John Wesley and the Eighteenth Century: A Study of His Social and Political Influence* (London: George Allen & Unwin, 1933), pp. 181-82; J. D. Thompson, *John Wesley as a Social Reformer* (New York: Eaton and Mains, 1898), pp. 24-29. See also Alan D. Gilbert's *Religion and Society in Industrial England* (London: Longmans, 1976).

41. Woodson, quoted by William Raspberry in "Neighborhood Healers," *Washington Post,* 18 September 1992.

soul than the pocketbook."[42] But are there enough charismatic leaders in the black community? Is there enough spiritual hunger so that messengers of hope will be able to redeem more than a few individuals? I do not know the answer to these questions, but Woodson most likely is right in insisting that only a truly religious appeal will be successful in bringing about moral renewal.

Religion and Morality: A Personal Assessment

"What ails modern civilization?" Russell Kirk asked in a lecture several years ago. "Fundamentally," he answered, "our society's affliction is the decay of religious belief. If a culture is to survive and flourish, it must not be severed from the religious vision out of which it arose. The high necessity of reflective men and women, then, is to labor for the restoration of religious teachings as a credible body of doctrine."[43] The issue raised here is not the theoretical question of whether individuals can be moral without religion; most religious thinkers agree that there can be justifications for morality other than religion and that religious training or belief does not guarantee morally commendable conduct. Nor is it the case that most Christians are moral only because of their fear of God or hellfire. There is the often-told story of the Catholic priest who said to a pair of well-behaved atheists, "I can't understand you boys; if I didn't believe in God I should be having a high old time." The priest of this story clearly represents a caricature rather than a typical Christian believer. What Kirk is asserting is that our culture cannot maintain its moral integrity unless religious belief once again becomes a constituent part of its intellectual foundation. Such a change, one wants to add, requires more than attendance at church services — it calls for true religiousness and not merely membership in a religious institution.

Kirk's insistence on the importance of religion for restoring the moral health of our society cannot easily be given empirical confirmation. Yet despite the problematic character of all such sweeping historical appraisals, I find Kirk's assertion plausible. Today, as in the past, religious beliefs and religious differences continue to contribute to the vicious hatred and violence that afflict societies as far apart as India and

42. Finn, "When Families Fail," *First Things*, January 1991, p. 23.
43. Kirk, "Civilization without Religion," lecture delivered at the Heritage Foundation, Washington, D.C., 24 July 1992.

the former Yugoslavia. At the same time, paradoxically, religion also acts as a crucial force inspiring moral conduct. The fact that some individuals manage to lead moral lives without belief in God refutes a strict and literal reading of Dostoyevsky's saying that without God everything is permitted.[44] But a weaker version of Dostoyevsky's thesis may nevertheless be true: a society that tries to cut itself off from the religious roots of its moral heritage is doomed to moral decline.

Back in 1944, the Quaker theologian David Elton Trueblood expressed his concern about the moral decay of his time and attributed it to the loss of theistic conviction. Ours, he warned, is a cut-flower civilization. "Beautiful as cut flowers may be, and much as we may use our ingenuity to keep them looking fresh for a while, they will eventually die, and they die because they are severed from their sustaining roots."[45] I believe that Trueblood's point is only slightly overstated. The moral crisis of our day has many causes, among them such prosaic facts as the rapidly growing number of female-headed households and the increase in the number of families in which both parents work. When such parents have less time to spend with their children and to monitor their moral development, the consequences cannot but be negative. Still, the modern spirit of secularism is probably one of the more corrosive elements in this matrix of interlocking factors. The willingness of modern man to challenge tradition and encrusted custom has had liberating consequences, but it has also exacted a heavy price. Contrary to the expectations of the Enlightenment, freeing individuals from the shackles of traditional religion does not result in their moral uplift. For some time now, Richard Weaver writes in his book *Ideas Have Consequences*, "every man has been not only his own priest but his own professor of ethics, and the consequence is an anarchy which threatens even that minimum of consensus of value necessary to the political state."[46] Many people, notes the philosopher William Frankena, "are thoughtless, selfish, irresponsible, lazy, mean, cruel, vicious or wicked."[47] There is no need to embrace the pessimism

44. See Dostoyevsky's *The Brothers Karamazov*, trans. Constance Garnett (New York: Modern Library, 1937), p. 629.

45. Trueblood, *The Predicament of Modern Man* (New York: Harper and Brothers, 1944), pp. 59-60.

46. Weaver, *Ideas Have Consequences* (Chicago: University of Chicago Press, 1984), p. 2.

47. Frankena, *Thinking about Morality* (Ann Arbor, Mich.: University of Michigan Press, 1980), p. 36.

of Augustinian theology in order to conclude that the Enlightenment's hope for human moral perfection is utterly utopian.

Society needs a morality that will curb the antisocial tendencies of human beings, and this morality cannot be taught simply on the rational grounds that it is socially necessary. No society has yet been successful in teaching morality without religion, for morality cannot be created. It requires the support of tradition, and this tradition is generally linked to religious precepts.[48] Certainly in the eyes of the great majority of the American people, morality is inseparably connected to religion — the moral rules are seen as God-given and derived from religion — and this connection yields concrete results. For example, according to a recent study, Americans who know the story of the Good Samaritan are far more likely than those ignorant of the parable to be involved in charitable activities, donate their time to voluntary organizations, care for someone who is sick, give money to a charity, and so on. We cannot be absolutely sure what came first — knowing the story or becoming involved in charitable causes — but since people in this survey often mentioned learning the story of the Good Samaritan as children, it is likely that it is indeed knowledge of the story that encourages compassion.[49]

People come to know of the Good Samaritan in churches where sermons about the parable are preached; in this way the churches play a crucial role in nourishing and replenishing the moral capital of our society. Those inclined to doubt the important role played by religion in upholding the moral order may want to confront the question posed by Dennis Prager, a Jewish writer and editor in Los Angeles: Imagine that you are walking alone at night down a dark alley in a bad neighborhood in Los Angeles, and you see several strapping young men walking toward you. Would you or would you not be relieved to know that they had just attended a Bible class? It is a sure bet, Prager maintains, that "even if you are a member of Atheists United, if you are a member of Down with God, Inc., you, too, would breathe a major sigh of relief if you were walking in a dark alley and you knew they had just been studying Genesis. Because while it is possible they will

---

48. See the suggestive discussion by Irving Kristol in "The Future of American Jewry," *Commentary*, August 1991, pp. 21-26.

49. The survey in question was done by Robert Wuthnow and is reported in his book entitled *Acts of Compassion: Caring for Others and Helping Ourselves* (Princeton, N.J.: Princeton University Press, 1991), p. 161.

mug or rape you, deep in your gut you know that the likelihood is that they won't."[50]

America is not unique in exhibiting a close connection between morality and religion. We know of no society anywhere that has managed to build a culture devoid of religion. Since the days of Neanderthal man, humans have practiced the ceremonial burying of their dead — a religious ritual that expresses grief and concern for the well-being of the departed. In primitive societies, customs and mores are regarded as ordained by supernatural beings; moral rules are obeyed at least in part out of fear of supernatural sanctions. In ancient Greek society, the sanctity of the oath, originally a religious idea, became the main source of the secular ideal of truthfulness. Religion has often been responsible for cruel strife and inhumanity, but it has also served as a basis for moral values and ideals, as a source of moral wisdom. Religious traditions have transmitted visions of the good life and have preserved people's collective moral experience. By building upon the idea that the gods or God protect and reward the good and punish the wicked and in numerous other ways, religion has shaped and interacted with people's moral life.

The great universal religions in particular have taught the virtues of disinterested goodwill, social responsibility, and individual moral integrity, without which no society can flourish. For much of this century, Sweden has been able to live under a highly secular ethos without experiencing substantial social dislocation. However, Sweden is a homogeneous society with a strong pietist tradition — a society, moreover, that has been the beneficiary of several centuries of socialization by the Lutheran Church. Whether this effect can last forever is questionable.[51] We know that in all Western countries the transformation of religious faith from public ethos into private affair — what Richard Neuhaus has called the dilemma of the "naked public square" — has created problems for the socialization of children. "Without the reinforcement of religious apprehensions," sociologist Bryan Wilson has observed, "moral guidance by teachers, or even by parents, has become difficult to provide. Consensus has gone, and the assumption

50. Dennis Prager and Jonathan Glover, "Can We Be Moral without God? A Debate at Oxford University," *Ultimate Issues* 9 (1993): 4.

51. See David Popenoe, *Disturbing the Nest: Family Change and Decline in Modern Societies* (New York: Aldine de Gruyter, 1988), pp. 157-59, 226-27, 311-19.

of public support for a distinctive moral code has disappeared."[52] Secularization has created a dangerous uncertainty about morals. As we have seen, the consequences of the new do-your-own-thing morality are especially severe for those at the bottom of society.

Not only is it true that morality cannot be created on the basis of the individual's alleged moral autonomy, but for the great majority of people morality cannot command conviction without being linked to some transcendent reasons for goodness. Not surprisingly, therefore, the notion of God has often recapitulated the basic notions of moral goodness in a society; belief in God has provided an absolute principle capable of grounding and integrating human values. Religion, by explicating the nature and purpose of human beings, places ultimate values in a context that awakens awe and reverence.[53] A few intellectuals may seek moral self-sufficiency, but most people cannot live that way. "We need faith in an ideal person," writes Erwin Goodenough, "not only as one who tells us what we may or may not do, but who, for all his strictness, loves us and forgives us and is willing and able to help us. For the gift of love and the gift of grace and strength are the same."[54] God's love and forgiveness, affirmed in the Bible, provide believers with an infusion of moral strength they could not achieve by their own efforts.

As insights provided by psychology and sociology confirm, the fundamental teachings of Christianity can be a source of moral empowerment. The great contribution of Christianity, as Paul Johnson has emphasized, has been to invest humans with a conscience and bid them follow it: "As an exercise in perfectionism, Christianity cannot succeed, even by its internal definitions; what it is designed to do is to set targets and standards, raise aspirations, to educate, stimulate and inspire."[55] The very impossibility of fulfilling the command to love your neighbor as yourself creates the kind of internal unrest that spurs some individuals to ever-greater moral exertion. Theological themes such as the sacredness and essential dignity of human life can

52. Wilson, *Religion in Sociological Perspective* (New York: Oxford University Press, 1982), p. 87.

53. See Osmond G. Ramberan, "Morality and Religion: An Analytical Approach with Implications for Religious Education," *Religious Humanism* 72 (1977): 527.

54. Goodenough, *Toward a Mature Faith* (New Haven: Yale University Press, 1955), p. 157.

55. Johnson, *A History of Christianity* (New York: Atheneum, 1977), p. 516.

help sensitize believers to values they might otherwise ignore. Indeed, even non-Christians and nonbelievers can have their thinking directed toward transcendent reference points and their moral concern raised by these teachings. The contributions made by Christian thinkers are particularly notable in regard to moral problems that involve the meaning of life and death. Christian traditions see these difficult dilemmas from a viewpoint other than immediate self-interest. Existential human problems such as suffering and death are approached from perspectives not generally addressed and invoked by secular bioethics; in this way religious discourse enriches our moral imagination and opens up important new moral horizons. For example, Christians believe in seeking to protect the weak and affirming the preciousness of human life, irrespective of whether it be nascent or developed into what some call "personhood." Anyone, whether Christian or non-Christian, who shares these beliefs cannot accept abortion on demand and agree to the view espoused by some secular humanists that abortion is morally right per se.

The Christian story can inspire other moral imperatives. It can overcome human weakness and awaken altruistic solicitude for others. A study of individuals who rescued Jews in Nazi-occupied Europe, mentioned earlier,[56] revealed that a large percentage of these rescuers unhesitatingly took enormous risks because they had internalized the Christian command to help those in need. Seeking to return to the New Testament ideal of selfless giving, many Christians tend to the poor and downtrodden. Because of the Christian concern for those in pain and suffering, monks, nuns, and other deeply religious individuals throughout history have flocked to the healing professions. For them, the practice of medicine has been a truly Christian vocation; they have realized that healers must think not only of curing but of caring. It is probably no accident that a large number of scholars who today are working in the field of medical ethics are Christians. Some of the most seminal contributions to this discipline have come from the ranks of Christian theologians.

It is possible to support the value of life on secular grounds, but the fact remains that few secular humanists are found among those defending unborn life or warning against the dangers of euthanasia. It is possible to be concerned for the poor and sick on the basis of a

---

56. Samuel and Pearl M. Oliner, *The Altruistic Personality: Rescuers of Jews in Nazi Europe* (New York: Free Press, 1988).

naturalist ethic, but adherents of this philosophy are not likely to produce a Dorothy Day or a Mother Teresa. Many of these people love humanity but not individual human beings with all their failings and shortcomings. They will be found participating in demonstrations for causes such as nuclear disarmament but not sitting at the bedside of a dying person. An ethic of moral autonomy and individual rights, so important to secular liberals, is incapable of sustaining or nourishing values such as altruism and self-sacrifice. There exists no secular counterpart to the Order of the Missionaries of Charity, founded by Mother Teresa, which today has almost 5,000 members seeking to meet the needs of the crippled and diseased in one hundred countries. The Christian injunction to care for those in need, reinforced by the inspiration and fellowship that are provided by the church as an on-going community, has produced results no secular ethic has been able to match. Christians conceive of the moral life as obedience to a divine intention, and this belief increases their willingness to act on the moral teachings of their creed. Even when theological teachings do not suggest novel moral principles, they do provide sources of motivation far stronger and with far greater effects on large numbers of people than reasoned philosophical discourse about duties and obligations. There are nonbelievers who engage in morally praiseworthy deeds, but it should be remembered that their conduct is considered praiseworthy because it is the sort of conduct that has been prescribed by the Judeo-Christian norm that by now is an implicit part of our moral tradition.

If, as we have seen, much of organized Christianity today no longer provides an effective counterforce to the destructive elements of modernity, most secular philosophy does not even recognize the problems. Some philosophers are engaged in dilemma ethics, the discussion of extreme situations far removed from the moral concerns of everyday life. Utilitarianism has a proud record of successfully criticizing existing institutions and beliefs, but today it is often engaged in cost-benefit calculations that blunt moral sensibility. It is only since the late 1960s and early 1970s that the new field of bioethics has restored to philosophy some of the human relevance it lost during the days of conceptual analysis.

Other philosophers remain preoccupied with the analysis of moral language and the subjectivity of moral judgments, and thus fail to address the crucial question of how we can make ourselves morally better. Most of the disputes about the nature of moral language, I would argue, are not only unresolvable but also largely irrelevant. In a conversation with the positivist Friedrich Waissmann that took place in 1929 in Vienna, Wittgenstein opposed what he called chatter *(Geschwätz)* about ethics — "whether there is knowledge in ethics, whether there are values, whether the Good can be defined, etc."[57] For Wittgenstein it was the deed, the actual manner of life, that was primary, and I believe that this is a correct view. To be moral is certainly more than to know principles and rules of right conduct. Most of our moral failings are the result of moral indifference, weakness of will, and/or self-indulgent habits — consequences of defects of character. "The hard part of morality, in short," William Kilpatrick has rightly noted, "is not *knowing* what is right but *doing* it."[58] The remedy for the deficit in moral conviction will not come from philosophy. As William Hudson, himself a philosopher, has argued, "If a team is playing football badly, what it needs is not more people who know the rules (every well-informed spectator does), but some better players. Similarly, if a society is deteriorating morally, what it needs is not more moral philosophers, but more good men."[59]

Finally, there are the secular humanists, committed to a selfish and hedonistic individualism. As we saw in an earlier chapter, secular humanists reduce ethical issues such as sexual morality, abortion, and the use of drugs to issues of civil liberties. They show no awareness that doing right is more important than exercising rights. They herald the toleration of destructive behavior as a blow struck on behalf of personal freedom. They turn moral relativism into a protective umbrella for all kinds of eccentricities, not to say moral depravities. Seeking to free us from what they regard as the encrusted moral beliefs of the past, they plead for the need to tolerate different lifestyles, including those that champion the fulfillment of unrestrained impulses and other destructive kinds of behavior. Many of them support the teaching of values clarification in our public schools, an educational approach that undermines traditional values and weakens the moral

57. *Wittgenstein und der Wiener Kreis,* ed. B. F. McGuiness (Oxford: Basil Blackwell, 1967), pp. 68-69, quoted by James C. Edwards in *Ethics without Philosophy: Wittgenstein and the Moral Life* (Gainesville, Fla.: University Presses of Florida, 1982), p. 94.

58. Kilpatrick, *Why Johnny Can't Tell Right from Wrong* (New York: Simon & Schuster, 1992), p. 88.

59. Hudson, *Modern Moral Philosophy* (Garden City, N.Y.: Anchor Books, 1970), pp. 17-18.

fiber of young people. The acceptance of moral pluralism can easily degenerate into the notion that all moral distinctions are relative.

Christian thinkers are right in warning about the negative consequences of moral relativism. Not so long ago some pacifists, worried about the danger that militant anticommunism could lead to war with the Soviet Union, argued that we had to understand the unique historical developments that had shaped the thinking of the Soviet people and that we had no right to impose our values on them. Some anthropologists maintain to this day that people should be allowed to live in accordance with their own customs, and that we must respect cultural differences. It is, of course, contradictory to assert, on the one hand, that there is no right or wrong apart from what a given society chooses to regard as right or wrong, and on the other hand to insist that it is wrong for people in one society to condemn or to interfere with the values or conduct of another society. One cannot in the same breath use "wrong" in both a relative and a nonrelative sense.[60] More important, to elevate to the highest good the notion that people should be allowed to live in accordance with their own customs, no matter how iniquitous and brutal, shows a callous disregard for other values that surely deserve a higher place in the value hierarchy.[61] Must we be tolerant of cannibalism or lynching or pogroms against Jews just because these practices and the belief systems from which they derive have deep historical roots in certain societies?

In the face of the vulgar relativism and cynicism that pervade modern society, it should be stated firmly: There are *some* moral truths. There are some moral norms that for all practical purposes are exceptionless and that can be considered self-evident. It is difficult to doubt that it is immoral to torture people for the amusement of others or to rape a mentally impaired minor girl. We know these actions to be morally repugnant, monstrous, and unacceptable just as surely as we know anything at all, and this knowledge is neither dependent upon faith in God nor culture-bound. The person who fails to recognize the immorality of such conduct, we are inclined to say, is morally incompetent and lacks a normal moral sense; he or she is like a color-blind person who is unable to distinguish red from green.

60. Bernard A. O. Williams, *Morality: An Introduction to Ethics* (New York: Harper & Row, 1972), p. 22.

61. See Shia Moser, *Absolutism and Relativism in Ethics* (Springfield, Ill.: Charles C. Thomas, 1968), p. 185.

Secular humanists also continue the Enlightenment project of seeking to free individuals from the shackles of traditional religion. They ostensibly wish to promote the sway of rationality, but their attacks on religion are so strident and shrill that they repel even would-be sympathizers. Yale professor Louis Dupré refused to sign the *Humanist Manifesto II* of 1973 because of its antireligious slogans and its questioning of the theistic roots of humanism.[62] John P. Roche and Karl Popper, well-known secular thinkers, declined to subscribe to the "Secular Humanist Declaration" of 1981, which they maintained was dogmatic as well as lacking intellectual modesty and a consciousness of human fallibility.[63]

Altogether, secular humanism as a consciously articulated philosophy remains the province of a small number of individuals. Today their shallow atheism has few supporters even in the intellectual community. As Paul Tillich suggested several decades ago, the main reason for this is to be found in a changed reality: "History has become the scene of a continuous chain of catastrophes, and thought has become an interpretation of the human predicament as manifest in these catastrophes, partly because they actually happened. . . . The picture of man as the master not only of nature but also of his personality and his society and therefore of his individual and historical destiny, this shining picture took on darker and darker colors. Destiny proved to be the master of man, not as a strange power but as power in the depth of man himself."[64] With regard to the moral disarray of our domestic society, too, there is a growing recognition that we must reaffirm concepts such as guilt and perhaps even sin. "I believe there is 'sin,'" psychiatrist Karl Menninger wrote, "which is expressed in ways which cannot be subsumed under verbal artifacts such as 'crime,' 'disease,' 'delinquency.' There *is* immorality; there *is* unethical behavior; there *is* wrongdoing."[65] Small wonder that in this kind of historical situation, the optimistic secularism favored by secular humanists has few takers.

62. Dupré, "The New Humanist Manifesto," *Commonweal*, 19 October 1973, pp. 55-58.
63. Statements by Roche and Popper are reproduced in the Spring 1981 issue of *Free Inquiry*.
64. Tillich, "Religion and the Intellectuals," *Partisan Review* 17 (1950): 254.
65. Menninger, *Whatever Became of Sin?* (New York: Hawthorn Books, 1973), p. 46.

Philosopher R. M. Hare, a Christian sympathetic to humanist ideals, refuses to call himself a humanist because it involves the risk that he will "be thought to be supporting, if not some kind of moral nihilism, at any rate a morality without visible means of support."[66] There are many people who share Hare's reservations about contemporary humanism but who, because they are adherents of other religious faiths or because they are nontheists, remain outside the Christian churches. For several good reasons, these two groups should join forces in the struggle for a more wholesome cultural future, to work to bring about a reversal of the ethos of radical individualism that threatens the moral integrity of our society. Both groups realize and appreciate the fact that it is the Judeo-Christian heritage which nurtures and replenishes the moral capital of our society. Both, aware of the moral cost of secularization and the weakening of our basic sense of social obligation, deplore the inroads of what has been called the "culture of narcissism," an outlook on life that makes self-fulfillment the supreme value. Both reject the snide attacks on religion carried out by militant secularists.

Cooperation between Christians and non-Christians in the task of achieving moral renewal is consistent with the demand of Vatican Council II "that all men, believers and unbelievers alike, ought to work for the rightful betterment of this world in which all alike live."[67] Such an alliance is also implicit in the fundamental insight of Saint Thomas Aquinas that natural law is a law of reason accessible to all; it involves basic moral norms that are cogent and convincing to everyone of goodwill. Paul Ramsey, the highly esteemed Protestant theologian, spoke of a convergence of Christian and humanist ethics, bringing together Christians and those for whom "the stern and moral voice of conscience occupies the place . . . traditionally reserved for the commandments of God."[68] A call for cooperation has also been issued by the evangelical theologian Carl Henry, who extends an invitation to humanists and others to join the struggle against the secularist currents

66. Hare, "The Simple Believer," in *Religion and Morality: A Collection of Essays,* ed. Gene Outka and John P. Reeder (Garden City, N.Y.: Doubleday, 1973), p. 425.
67. "Pastoral Constitution on the Church in the Modern World" *(Gaudium et Spes),* sec. 21, in Walter M. Abbott, ed., *The Documents of Vatican II* (New York: America Press, 1966), p. 219.
68. Ramsey, *Ethics and the Edges of Life: Medical and Legal Intersections* (New Haven, Conn.: Yale University Press, 1978), p. 81.

of modernity "even if their alien and contrabiblical philosophies seem to many of us unpromising."[69] Finally, there is a prudential argument for such a joint effort. The philosopher William Frankena has pointed out that the ethics of Jesus are compatible with a variety of meta-ethical theories (theories that justify moral beliefs), and that morality needs all the help it can get.[70] In a recent article, Robert Bork has warned against forgoing cooperation between Christians and those who do not anchor their values in a transcendent order, for, as he put it, "We have few enough allies without thinning the ranks further."[71]

The battle against the current law on abortion is an example of a struggle in which such cooperation could lead to important consequences. The acceptance of abortion on demand involves a rejection of the most profound principles of human morality, for the overriding value of life is found in the ethical traditions of all human societies. It is not a sectarian tenet. "Do no harm" is a fundamental code for physicians, religious or nonreligious. The intrinsic value of human life is upheld by Christians, Jews, Muslims, Buddhists, and humanists; it should be of concern even to atheists. In 1979, Bernard Nathanson, at the time a self-confessed nonbeliever, put it this way: "Even if God does not exist, the fetus does."[72]

There is solid evidence that a majority of the American people repudiate the unqualified right to an abortion established by *Roe v. Wade* and *Doe v. Bolton*. What would command wide support is a moderate, restrictive public policy that rejects abortion on demand but allows it in cases of rape, incest, a severe threat to the health of the mother, or a grave fetal deformity. According to some estimates, such a policy would prohibit 95 percent of abortions carried out in this country today. Here is a chance to develop a moral consensus in the bitter and polarized abortion debate.

The theoretical disagreement over the value and the rights of the fetus probably will never be resolved to the satisfaction of all the

---

69. Henry, *The Christian Mindset in a Secular Society: Promoting Evangelical Renewal and National Righteousness* (Portland, Ore.: Multnomah Press, 1984), p. 80.

70. Frankena, "The Potential of Theology for Ethics," in *Theology and Bioethics: Exploring the Foundations and Frontiers,* ed. Earl E. Shelp (Dordrecht: D. Reidel, 1985), p. 63. See also Frankena's essay entitled "Love and Principle in Christian Ethics," in *Faith and Philosophy: Philosophical Studies in Religion and Ethics,* ed. Alvin Plantinga (Grand Rapids, Mich.: Wm. B. Eerdmans, 1964), p. 225.

71. Bork, "Natural Law and the Constitution," *First Things,* March 1992, p. 20.

72. Nathanson, *Aborting America* (Garden City, N.Y.: Doubleday, 1979), p. 176.

parties involved in the dispute over abortion. However, by making some effort and by avoiding the absolutizing of moral principles, it should be possible to move beyond the view that the fetus either counts as nothing or counts as much as any adult. Such a compromise will have to be built upon the recognition that life is precious but not the only value to be treasured. It will have to concede that in some tragic situations abortion could be defended as a morally justified act, just as we now defend killing in self-defense and the destruction of innocent life in a just war. This kind of compromise is urgently needed, for, left unchecked, the tendency to solve life-and-death dilemmas by strictly utilitarian and functional criteria could lead to a serious weakening of the respect for life that all sides affirm as valuable. A society that accepts abortion on demand is a society that some day may accept the killing of comatose adults, the severely psychotic, and other vulnerable and helpless groups of human beings.

Many Americans are wary of Protestant groups, such as the former Moral Majority and Pat Robertson's Christian Coalition, that seek a revival of biblical values. They point to the charlatans who serve as preachers in some fundamentalist churches, and they worry about the triumphalism and intolerance often found among the religious right. These fears are not entirely unjustified, but a strengthening of Christian values in our society need not lead to censorship, repression, or a break with the valuable tradition of the separation between church and state.

Arguing against the pretensions of some elements in the religious right, Carl Henry and many other Christian thinkers have stressed that it would be unconstitutional as well as wrong to impose a Christian morality upon non-Christians. Civil government defines what is unlawful, not what is sinful. "Freedom to sin," Henry argues, "is a necessary component of life in a fallen society." Religious freedom is an indispensable treasure that must not be jeopardized in the debate over values. "An earthly society in which man is free to choose atheism," Henry maintains, "is better than one in which he is compelled to choose theism." The Christian objective should be to "support legislation that provides for all citizens the freedom to persuade others to recognize what is right and to do it, and to advance and support programs that coincide with what we believe a just society must champion."[73] Values are to be legislated not because they conform to theo-

73. Henry, *The Christian Mindset in a Secular Society*, pp. 122, 124, 59.

logical assumptions or private truths but because they are widely shared and can be defended by arguments that are public in character. "Those who want to bring religiously based values to bear in public discourse," Richard Neuhaus has maintained, "have an obligation to 'translate' those values into terms that are as accessible as possible to those who do not share the same religious grounding."[74]

Many Christians find any reference to the social utility of the Christian religion condescending and patronizing. They feel that a religion which believes in two worlds and the crucial importance of salvation cannot be judged by the value of its fruits here on earth. If the Christian religion is true, its fruits are good fruits even if in this world they should prove ill adapted and unsuitable. "To justify Christianity because it provides a foundation for morality, instead of showing the necessity of Christian morality from the truth of Christianity," argued T. S. Eliot, "is a very dangerous inversion."[75] In fact, however, Christians need not choose between the truth and the social usefulness of their religion. As a recent statement by a group of American conservative Roman Catholics and evangelicals put it, "To propose that securing civil virtue is the purpose of religion is blasphemous. To deny that securing civil virtue is a benefit of religion is blindness."[76]

Writing in the 1850s, John Stuart Mill suggested that the "utility of religion did not need to be asserted until the arguments for its truth had in a great measure ceased to convince." It was only in an "age of weak beliefs" that people had to be admonished to be religious.[77] However, Mill may have idealized the past. As Alfred North Whitehead has suggested, humankind has always experienced loss of religious faith.[78] What basis do we have for the widespread assumption that the Middle Ages were an age of faith? Dissatisfaction with the present often leads to nostalgia for the past, and this past may have been no

74. Neuhaus, *The Naked Public Square: Religion and Democracy in America* (Grand Rapids, Mich.: Wm. B. Eerdmans, 1984), p. 125.

75. Eliot, "The Idea of a Christian Society," in *Christianity and Culture* (New York: Harcourt Brace Jovanovich, 1968), p. 46.

76. "Evangelicals and Catholics Together: The Christian Mission in the Third Millennium," *First Things*, no. 43 (May 1994), p. 18.

77. Mill, "Utility of Religion," in *Three Essays on Religion* (London: Longman, Green, Reader and Dyer, 1874), p. 70. The same point is made by Herbert J. Muller in *Religion and Freedom in the Modern World* (Chicago: University of Chicago Press, 1963), p. 34.

78. Whitehead, *Science and the Modern World* (New York: Macmillan, 1927), p. 297.

better than the present. Certainly the Middle Ages, whether an age of faith or not, had their share of brutality and cruelty. If there is a difference between earlier periods of moral depravity and modern decadence, it is that previously Christian values were largely unchallenged and most people felt guilty about doing evil. This consensus no longer exists today, and we now have elaborate theories that justify what is manifestly immoral conduct.

According to Leszek Kolakowski, it is "an inconsistent, manipulative spirit" that makes modern intellectuals dwell on the importance of Christianity for human morality and warn of the dangers of secularism:

> There is something alarmingly desperate in intellectuals who have no religious attachment, faith or loyalty proper, but who insist on the irreplaceable educational and moral role of religion in our world and deplore its fragility — to which they themselves bear witness. I do not blame them either for being irreligious or for asserting the crucial value of religious experience. I simply cannot persuade myself that their work might produce changes they believe desirable: because in order to spread faith, faith is needed, and not an intellectual assertion of the social utility of faith.[79]

Kolakowski may be correct in thinking that only priests or prophets and not secular intellectuals can be expected to bring about the kind of moral renovation needed today. Indeed, I am not at all sure that even the powerful exertions of charismatic figures will succeed in reversing the destructive cultural trends in which we find ourselves caught. And yet I am also enough of an antihistoricist and optimist to believe that we humans make our own history and are not doomed to be prisoners of some inevitable destiny. The tremendous changes in deep-seated attitudes about racial equality, the status of women, and the importance of the environment that this country has experienced during the last thirty years or so can serve as a reminder that cultural transformations can be achieved. "Revival and reformation in America in the late twentieth century," a thoughtful British observer of intellectual trends in the United States has pointed out, "have about as much chance as the likelihood of an obscure provincial sect overturning Imperial Rome, or of a shipload of motley Lincolnshire dropouts found-

79. Kolakowski, "Modernity on Endless Trial," *Encounter*, March 1986, p. 11.

ing the twentieth century's greatest superpower."[80] Throughout its history, American society has been able to maintain its dynamic momentum and capacity for change. For this reason I think the joint struggle of believers and nonbelievers for cultural renewal is worth undertaking. There is nothing to lose and much to gain.

I flatter myself that I do not fit the picture of the intellectual drawn by Kolakowski in the above quotation. While I have neither a religious affiliation nor a religious faith in the traditional sense of that term, I do have strong moral convictions as well as loyalties. The faith upon which I draw in my moral reasoning lacks a theistic component, but this deficiency, in my view, is of no moral significance; religious believers do not have a monopoly on moral ideals and beliefs. I am an agnostic, but the fact that I strongly affirm some of the most basic moral precepts of the Judeo-Christian tradition will hopefully dispel any notion that I appreciate religion only because of its social utility — a pragmatic approach that believers justifiably find objectionable. I admire my religious friends, many of whom, on account of their religious belief, probably are better human beings than I manage to be. I share the sentiment of the British scientist and nobel laureate Peter Medawar, also a nonbeliever, who has expressed the wish that his "behavior — short of overt acts of worship or the avowal of beliefs I do not hold — . . . be such that people take me for a religious man in respect of helpfulness, considerateness and other evidences of an inclination to make the world better than it otherwise would be."[81]

Unlike my religious friends, I am not drawn to prayer. I am also a rationalist of sorts. I believe in the power of human reason to conquer adversities and improve the human condition. But reason alone, as I have argued in this book, is clearly not enough to provide moral inspiration. Moral reasoning can inform a conscience; it cannot create one. At the same time, I am quite sure that the abandonment of reason is a sure road to disaster. Many Christian thinkers share this view. I hope that together we can make a difference.

80. Os Guinness, The American Hour: America's Time of Reckoning and the Once and Future Role of Faith (New York: Free Press, 1993), pp. 414-15.

81. Medawar, The Limits of Science (New York: Harper & Row, 1984), p. 96.

Selected Bibliography

Acton, John Emerich Edward Dalberg. *Essays on Freedom and Power.* London: Thames & Hudson, 1956.

Allport, Gordon W. *The Person in Psychology: Selected Essays.* Boston: Beacon Press, 1968.

Anscombe, G. E. M. *Ethics, Religion, and Politics.* Minneapolis: University of Minnesota Press, 1981.

Argyle, Michael, and Benjamin Beit-Hallahmi. *The Social Psychology of Religion.* London: Routledge & Kegan Paul, 1975.

Baelz, Peter R. *Ethics and Belief.* New York: Seabury Press, 1977.

Banfield, Edward C. *The Unheavenly City Revisited.* Boston: Little, Brown, 1974.

Barrett, Cyril. *Wittgenstein on Ethics and Religious Belief.* Oxford: Basil Blackwell, 1991.

Bellah, Robert N., et al. *Habits of the Heart: Individualism and Commitment in American Life.* New York: Harper & Row, 1986.

Bell, Daniel. *The Winding Passage.* Cambridge, Mass.: ABT Books, 1980.

Bennett, William J. *The Index of Leading Cultural Indicators: Facts and Figures on the State of American Society.* New York: Simon & Schuster, 1994.

Berger, Brigitte, and Peter L. Berger. *The War on the Family: Capturing the Middle Ground.* Garden City, N.Y.: Doubleday, 1983.

Berger, Peter L. *A Far Glory: The Quest for Faith in an Age of Credulity.* New York: Free Press, 1992.

Berger, Peter L., and Richard John Neuhaus. *To Empower People: The Role of Mediating Structures in Public Policy.* Washington, D.C.: American Enterprise Institute, 1977.

Berlin, Isaiah. *Four Essays on Liberty.* New York: Oxford University Press, 1969.

Blankenhorn, David, et al., eds. *Rebuilding the Nest: A New Commitment to the American Family.* Milwaukee: Family Service America, 1990.

Boswell, John. *The Kindness of Strangers: The Abandonment of Children in Western Europe from Late Antiquity to the Renaissance.* New York: Pantheon Books, 1988.

Bredvold, Louis I. *The Brave New World of the Enlightenment.* Ann Arbor, Mich.: University of Michigan Press, 1961.

Brinton, Crane. *A History of Western Morals.* New York: Harcourt, Brace, 1959.

Brody, Baruch A., ed. *Readings in the Philosophy of Religion: An Analytical Approach.* Englewood Cliffs, N.J.: Prentice Hall, 1974.

Bryk, Anthony S., et al. *Catholic Schools and the Common Good.* Cambridge, Mass.: Harvard University Press, 1993.

Burkert, Walter. *Greek Religion: Archaic and Classical.* Translated by John Raffan. Oxford: Basil Blackwell, 1985.

Butler, Jon. *Awash in a Sea of Faith: Christianizing the American People.* Cambridge, Mass.: Harvard University Press, 1990.

Butterfield, Herbert. *Christianity and History.* New York: Charles Scribner's Sons, 1950.

Callahan, Sidney, and Daniel Callahan. *Abortion: Understanding Differences.* New York: Plenum Press, 1984.

Carillo de Albornoz, Angel F. *Religious Liberty.* Translated by John Drury. New York: Sheed & Ward, 1967.

Carter, Stephen L. *The Culture of Disbelief: How American Law and Politics Trivialize Religious Devotion.* New York: Basic Books, 1993.

Chazan, Barry I. *Contemporary Approaches to Moral Education.* New York: Teachers College Press, 1985.

Christensen, Bryce J., ed. *The Retreat from Marriage: Causes and Consequences.* Lanham, Md.: University Press of America, 1990.

Cohen, I. Bernard, ed. *Puritanism and the Rise of Modern Science: The Merton Thesis.* New Brunswick, N.J.: Rutgers University Press, 1990.

Comstock, George. *Television in America.* 2d ed. Newbury Park, Calif.: Sage Publications, 1991.

Crocker, Lester G. *Nature and Culture: Ethical Thought in the French Enlightenment.* Baltimore: Johns Hopkins Press, 1963.

Davis, David Brion. *The Problem of Slavery in Western Culture*. Ithaca, N.Y.: Cornell University Press, 1966.

Dawson, Christopher. *Progress and Religion: A Historical Enquiry*. New York: Sheed & Ward, 1938.

———. *Religion and the Rise of Western Culture*. New York: Sheed & Ward, 1950.

Dewey, John. *A Common Faith*. New Haven, Conn.: Yale University Press, 1934.

Edwards, James C. *Ethics without Philosophy: Wittgenstein and the Moral Life*. Gainesville, Fla.: University Presses of Florida, 1982.

Edwards, Maldwyn. *John Wesley and the Eighteenth Century: A Study of His Social and Political Influence*. London: George Allen & Unwin, 1933.

Eliot, T. S. *Christianity and Culture*. New York: Harcourt Brace Jovanovich, 1968.

Finke, Roger, and Rodney Stark. *The Churching of America, 1776-1990: Winners and Losers in Our Religious Economy*. New Brunswick, N.J.: Rutgers University Press, 1992.

Flew, Antony. *The Presumption of Atheism*. New York: Barnes & Noble, 1976.

Frankel, Charles. *The Case for Modern Man*. Boston: Beacon Press, 1959.

Frankena, William K. *Thinking about Morality*. Ann Arbor, Mich.: University of Michigan Press, 1980.

Frazier, Edward Franklin. *The Negro Family in the United States*. Chicago: University of Chicago Press, 1966.

Freud, Sigmund. *Civilization and Its Discontents* and *The Future of an Illusion* in *Complete Psychological Works*, vol. 21. Translated by James Strachey. London: Hogarth Press, 1961.

Gallup, George H., Jr., and Jim Castelli. *The People's Religion: American Faith in the Nineties*. New York: Macmillan, 1989.

Gallup, George H., Jr., and Sarah Jones. *100 Questions and Answers: Religion in America*. Princeton, N.J.: Princeton Religion Research Center, 1989.

Gallup, George H., Jr., and Timothy Jones. *The Saints among Us*. Harrisburg, Pa.: Morehouse, 1992.

Garnett, Arthur Campbell. *Religion and the Moral Life*. New York: Ronald Press, 1955.

Gay, Peter. *The Enlightenment: An Interpretation*. 2 vols. New York: Alfred A. Knopf, 1966-1969.

————. *The Party of Humanity: Essays in the French Enlightenment.* New York: Alfred A. Knopf, 1964.

Gellner, Ernest. *Postmodernism, Reason, and Religion.* London: Routledge, 1992.

Glazer, Nathan. *The Limits of Social Policy.* Cambridge, Mass.: Harvard University Press, 1988.

Glock, Charles Y., and Rodney Stark. *Christian Belief and Anti-Semitism.* New York: Harper & Row, 1966.

Goodenough, Erwin R. *Toward a Mature Faith.* New Haven, Conn.: Yale University Press, 1955.

Goody, Jack. *The Development of the Family and Marriage in Europe.* Cambridge: Cambridge University Press, 1983.

Greeley, Andrew M. *Religious Change in America.* Cambridge, Mass.: Harvard University Press, 1989.

————. *Unsecular Man: The Persistence of Religion.* New York: Schocken Books, 1972.

Guinness, Os. *The American Hour: America's Time of Reckoning and the Once and Future Role of Faith.* New York: Free Press, 1993.

Gustafson, James M. *Can Ethics Be Christian?* Chicago: University of Chicago Press, 1975.

————. *Theology and Christian Ethics.* Philadelphia: Pilgrim Press, 1974.

Gutman, Amy. *Democratic Education.* Princeton, N.J.: Princeton University Press, 1987.

Gutman, Herbert G. *The Black Family in Slavery and Freedom: 1750-1925.* New York: Pantheon Books, 1976.

Hale, J. Russell. *The Unchurched: Who They Are and Why They Stay Away.* New York: Harper & Row, 1980.

Hallie, Philip H. *Lest Innocent Blood Be Shed: The Story of the Village of Le Chambon and How Goodness Happened There.* New York: Harper & Row, 1979.

Hanke, Lewis. *The Spanish Struggle for Justice in the Conquest of America.* Philadelphia: University of Pennsylvania Press, 1949.

Hauerwas, Stanley. *A Community of Character: Toward a Constructive Christian Social Ethic.* Notre Dame, Ind.: University of Notre Dame Press, 1981.

Henry, Carl F. H. *The Christian Mindset in a Secular Society: Promoting Evangelical Renewal and National Righteousness.* Portland, Ore.: Multnomah Press, 1984.

Herberg, Will. *Protestant — Catholic — Jew: An Essay in American Religious Sociology.* Garden City, N.Y.: Doubleday, 1960.

Hitchcock, James. *What Is Secular Humanism? Why Humanism Became Secular and How It Is Changing Our World.* Ann Arbor, Mich.: Servant Books, 1982.

Hook, Sidney. *The Place of Religion in a Free Society.* Lincoln, Neb.: University of Nebraska Press, 1967.

Hudson, William D. *Wittgenstein and Religious Belief.* New York: St. Martin's Press, 1975.

Hunter, James Davison. *American Evangelicalism: Conservative Religion and the Quandary of Modernity.* New Brunswick, N.J.: Rutgers University Press, 1983.

———. *Culture Wars: The Struggle to Define America.* New York: Basic Books, 1991.

Jencks, Christopher, and Paul E. Peterson, eds. *The Urban Underclass.* Washington, D.C.: Brookings Institution, 1991.

Johnson, Paul. *A History of Christianity.* New York: Atheneum, 1977.

Kaufman, Walter. *The Faith of a Heretic.* Garden City, N.Y.: Doubleday, 1961.

Kilpatrick, William K. *Why Johnny Can't Tell Right from Wrong.* New York: Simon & Schuster, 1992.

Kolakowski, Leszek. *Modernity on Endless Trial.* Chicago: University of Chicago Press, 1990.

———. *Religion.* New York: Oxford University Press, 1982.

Kosmin, Barry A., and Seymour Lachman. *One Nation under God: Religion in Contemporary American Society.* New York: Harmony Books, 1993.

Kurtz, Paul. *Eupraxophy: Living without Religion.* Buffalo, N.Y.: Prometheus Books, 1989.

———. *In Defense of Secular Humanism.* Buffalo, N.Y.: Prometheus Books, 1983.

Langmuir, Gavin I. *History, Religion, and Antisemitism.* Berkeley and Los Angeles: University of California Press, 1990.

Lecky, W. E. H. *History of European Morals from Augustus to Charlemagne.* New York: George Braziller, 1955.

———. *History of the Rise and Influence of the Spirit of Rationalism in Europe.* 2 vols. New York: D. Appleton, 1866.

Lincoln, C. Eric, and Lawrence H. Mamiya. *The Black Church in the African-American Experience.* Durham, N.C.: Duke University Press, 1990.

MacIntyre, Alasdair. *Secularization and Moral Change*. London: Oxford University Press, 1967.

Magnet, Myron. *The Dream and the Nightmare: The Sixties Legacy to the Underclass*. New York: William Morrow, 1993.

Martin, Thomas K., et al., eds. *Utah in Demographic Perspective: Regional and National Contrasts*. N.p.: Signature Press, 1986.

Marty, Martin E. *Varieties of Unbelief*. New York: Holt, Rinehart & Winston, 1964.

Mead, Lawrence M. *The New Politics of Poverty: The Nonworking Poor in America*. New York: Basic Books, 1992.

Merton, Robert K. *Science, Technology, and Society in Seventeenth-Century England*. New York: Howard Fertig, 1970.

Mill, John Stuart. *Three Essays on Religion*. London: Longmans, Green, Reader and Dyer, 1874.

Mitchell, Basil. *Morality, Religious and Secular: The Dilemma of the Traditional Conscience*. New York: Oxford University Press, 1980.

Moynihan, Daniel Patrick. *Family and Nation*. New York: Harcourt Brace Jovanovich, 1986.

Muller, Herbert J. *Religion and Freedom in the Modern World*. Chicago: University of Chicago Press, 1963.

Murray, Charles. *Losing Ground: American Social Policy, 1950-1980*. New York: Basic Books, 1984.

Nathanson, Bernard N. *Aborting America*. Garden City, N.Y.: Doubleday, 1979.

Natoli, Charles M. *Nietzsche and Pascal on Christianity*. New York: Peter Lang, 1985.

Neuhaus, Richard John. *The Naked Public Square: Religion and Democracy in America*. Grand Rapids, Mich.: Wm. B. Eerdmans, 1984.

————, ed. *Unsecular America*. Grand Rapids, Mich.: Wm. B. Eerdmans, 1986.

Niebuhr, Reinhold. *Does Civilization Need Religion? A Study in the Social Resources and Limitations of Religion in Modern Life*. New York: Macmillan, 1927.

Nielsen, Kai. *God and the Grounding of Morality*. Ottawa: University of Ottawa Press, 1991.

————. *Why Be Moral?* Buffalo, N.Y.: Prometheus Books, 1989.

Noonan, John T., Jr. *The Morality of Abortion: Legal and Historical Perspectives*. Cambridge, Mass.: Harvard University Press, 1970.

Novak, Michael. *A Community of Self-Reliance: The New Consensus on Family and Welfare*. Washington, D.C.: American Enterprise Institute, 1987.

Olasky, Marvin N. *The Tragedy of American Compassion*. Washington, D.C.: Regnery Gateway, 1992.

Oliner, Samuel. *The Altruistic Personality: Rescuers of Jews in Nazi Europe*. New York: Free Press, 1988.

Outka, Gene, and John P. Reeder, Jr., eds. *Religion and Morality: A Collection of Essays*. Garden City, N.Y.: Doubleday, 1973.

Popenoe, David. *Disturbing the Nest: Family Change and Decline in Modern Societies*. New York: Aldine de Gruyter, 1988.

Princeton Religion Research Center. *Religion in America: 1992-1993*. Princeton, N.J.: Princeton Religion Research Center, 1993.

Rainwater, Lee, and William L. Yancey. *The Moynihan Report and the Politics of Controversy*. Cambridge, Mass.: MIT Press, 1967.

Raths, Louis E., et al. *Values and Teaching: Working with Values in the Classroom*. 2d ed. Columbus, Ohio: Charles E. Merrill, 1978.

Reichley, A. James. *Religion in American Public Life*. Washington, D.C.: Brookings Institution, 1985.

Roof, Wade Clark, and William McKinney. *American Mainline Religion: Its Changing Shape and Future*. New Brunswick, N.J.: Rutgers University Press, 1987.

Russell, Bertrand. *Why I Am Not a Christian and Other Essays*. New York: Simon & Schuster, 1964.

Semmel, Bernard. *The Methodist Revolution*. New York: Basic Books, 1973.

Stark, Rodney, and William Sims Bainbridge. *The Future of Religion: Secularization, Revival, and Cult Formation*. Berkeley and Los Angeles: University of California Press, 1985.

Sykes, Charles J. *A Nation of Victims: The Decay of the American Character*. New York: St. Martin's Press, 1992.

Taylor, Charles. *Sources of the Self: The Making of the Modern Identity*. Cambridge, Mass.: Harvard University Press, 1989.

Trueblood, David Elton. *The Predicament of Modern Man*. New York: Harper & Brothers, 1944.

Weaver, Richard M. *Ideas Have Consequences*. Chicago: University of Chicago Press, 1984.

Westermarck, Edward. *Christianity and Morals*. London: Kegan Paul, 1939.

Whitehead, Alfred North. *Science and the Modern World*. New York: Macmillan, 1927.

Williams, James D., ed. *The State of Black America, 1986*. New York: National Urban League, 1986.

Wilson, Bryan. *Religion in Sociological Perspective*. New York: Oxford University Press, 1982.

Wilson, James Q., and Glenn C. Loury. *Families, Schools, and Delinquency Prevention*. New York: Springer, 1987.

Wilson, James Q., and Joan Petersilia. *Crime*. San Francisco: ICS Press, 1995.

Wilson, William Julius. *The Truly Disadvantaged: The Inner City, the Underclass, and Public Policy*. Chicago: University of Chicago Press, 1987.

Wuthnow, Robert. *The Restructuring of American Religion: Society and Faith since World War II*. Princeton, N.J.: Princeton University Press, 1988.

Index

THE RED MIND-SET 41

VALUE SHIFT 46

BREAK UP OF BLACK FAMILY 50f

UNDERCLASS 54, 56

INDUSTRIALISM, CAPITALISM, BUREAUCRACY 66

THE UNCHURCHED 71

CHURCH GOERS + PREJUDICE 102

INTEGRAL 125

RELIGION

CREDIBILITY/PLAUSIBILITY 144

a-morality 145